Superstar
Sales

SUPERSTAR SALES

A 31-DAY PLAN TO MOTIVATE PEOPLE, BUILD RAPPORT, AND CLOSE MORE SALES

RICK CONLOW
and

DOUG WATSABAUGH

CAREER PRESS

Pompton Plains, NJ

Superstar Sales
Edited by Jodi Brandon
Typeset by Eileen Munson
Printed in the U.S.A.

To order this title, please call toll-free 1-800-CAREER-1 (NJ and Canada: 201-848-0310) to order using VISA or MasterCard, or for further information on books from Career Press.

The Career Press, Inc.
220 West Parkway, Unit 12
Pompton Plains, NJ 07444
www.careerpress.com

Library of Congress Cataloging-in-Publication Data

CIP Data Available Upon Request.

Contents

Preface

S*uperstar Selling.* Really? Exactly what does that mean? Good questions. We'd like to answer them for you since you've picked up this book.

Yes, really. We believe that you are capable of becoming a Superstar sales professional. And, we believe this book can help you immensely, whether you are a new entry into the world of professional sales or you're an experienced veteran in this rapidly evolving and demanding profession.

This book is a close companion to our recently published book, *Superstar Leadership.* And, it is similar in this respect: We believe that both professions (leadership and sales) can be learned. We also believe that you'll never know all there is to know, and you will never possess all of the skills that are available to you—either as a leader or as a sales professional. At the same time, we have seen many professionals achieve remarkable levels of accomplishment and become true Superstars as a result of their constant search for improvement. They've achieved their success, not because they were born leaders or sales professionals, but as a result of constant practice and refinement of their skills and knowledge.

We all know, in theory, that the pace of change today absolutely demands that we become lifelong learners, and that we develop and practice new skills and approaches continuously. As a sales professional today, you are working in a world where the balance of knowledge and power has dramatically shifted toward your customer. Your selling efforts today begin with a customer who already has immediate access to a wealth of information about your product, its (and your) performance history, your pricing, your customers' complaints, your competition, and many other things that used to be known only by you. The challenge now is to move up the value chain and find additional ways to add value for your clients. The relationship is important, but customers expect much more from you today than they ever have in the past. You cannot rely on the same old skills and knowledge to develop and maintain productive relationships with your customers.

Superstar Sales is structured to take you through 31 days of learning, practice, and review of today's selling requirements. In our experience, it's not just what you know that makes you effective; it's what you do with what you know. Professional athletes practice on a daily basis to sharpen their game and renew their strengths. Similarly, you, as a sales professional, must constantly challenge your assumptions, review your use of the fundamentals, and look for new skills and insights that will give you an edge over your competition and help you to differentiate yourself from all of your competitors. *Superstar Sales* begins with a solid self-assessment and a description of the sales competencies that will equip you to perform at the highest levels in your profession. Next, you will read and work your way through a series of daily sessions that will provide focus, practice, and reinforcement for your skill and knowledge development.

We owe a debt of gratitude to the thousands of sales professionals we've worked with and learned from during our respective 35-plus years as sales professionals, trainers, and consultants. We've received training and coaching from some of the best trainers and practitioners in the world. We've observed and coached thousands as they've strived for and achieved excellence in their field. Much of what we've seen and learned has been distilled into the core ideas, insights, and lessons presented here. We wish you good luck, and we offer you all of our encouragement as you launch yourself into your next great learning adventure. We know it's not easy, but we strongly believe it's worth the effort. Welcome to the road to *Superstar Sales.* Work hard, stay focused on your customers, practice continuously, and you'll achieve great things!

Rick Conlow and Doug Watsabaugh
January 2013

How Good Can You Be?

How good can you be? Can you be a sales Superstar? Scientists estimate that the average human being uses less than 1 percent of his or her own potential. Scientists also note that over the course of our lifetime, we lose 1 percent of our potential. Now, we just need to make sure that the 1 percent we lose isn't the 1 percent we use.

Research indicates that ongoing learning and training help people tap into their potential. This means that you have a tremendous opportunity to achieve sales success. Unfortunately, too many salespeople use excuses, which ultimately cap their income and limit their results. There are seven common but deadly excuses that can be dangerous:

1. **I don't have time.** (They aren't organized!)
2. **Management doesn't support me.** (They blame their lack of results on management!)
3. **It's a tough world.** (They aren't prepared!)
4. **Price is the issue.** (They don't know the market well enough!)
5. **Customers don't understand.** (They're not aware of the customers' real needs!)
6. **It's a product problem.** (They aren't initiating enough conversation or needs analysis with potential customers!)
7. **It's unfair; the competition has the advantage.** (They aren't students of the game; they're stuck in a rut with outdated skills and approaches!)

The complaint list could continue, but the salespeople who grumble with these excuses are forgetting what President Harry S. Truman once said: "The buck stops here." If you are a salesperson, you are accountable and responsible for *your* results. *Period.* Obstacles are inevitable and usually difficult, so what are you going to do about it?

Put Your Energy Into the *Potential,* Not the Problem!

Cliff Miedl, a 20-year-old plumber's apprentice, accidentally drove his jackhammer through three high-voltage cables one day at work. His body instantly received 30,000 volts of electricity. That's 15 times the voltage delivered by an electric chair. The shock shattered his knees, exploded part of his skull, took off most of his toes, and left a hole in his back as the electricity left his body. Even though his heart stopped three times, Cliff survived. Doctors said he'd never walk again.

Through a slow and painful recovery, Cliff learned to walk again. Even further, he was inspired to start kayaking by Greg Barton, the 1988 kayak Olympian who managed to win two gold medals in spite of having two clubfeet. Cliff became so good that he made the U.S. Olympic team. At the 2000 Sydney Games, the 603 U.S. team members nominated Cliff to be the flag bearer for the opening ceremony march. Cliff turned a tragedy into a triumph.

Receiving 30,000 volts of electricity is hard. The road to recovery is hard. Product problems and customer complaints can also be hard, but not in comparison with Cliff's ordeal. Always believe in your potential—the things you can manage and control.

Do not waste time on things you can't do or can't control. Superstars have a persistent spirit and a can-do attitude that their clients love. The payoff is in the increased sales and income!

Be *Action-Oriented,* Not Apathetic!

According to research, salespeople are the single largest contributors to the customer's decision-making process during a purchase.[1] What an opportunity to make a difference! Too many salespeople react negatively to rejection. They quit and let events strain their spirit. Superstar salespeople think proactively and take action to elicit positive results. This isn't a cliché; it's a reality.

A few years ago, there was a story published about a man in the *Guinness Book of World Records.* He held the running record for completing 90 marathons in one year. In honor of the new millennium, he ran 200 marathons in the year 2000! When asked about his purpose for the adventure, he said that he didn't want anyone to break his record, and he knew he could do it. What an attitude! If you're not interested in adjusting your attitude and polishing your skills, how can you expect your customers to be convinced that working with you is the way to go?

Stay *Proactive*, Not Reactive!

All great achievers are great planners. Although you may not like paperwork or computers, you have to have a plan and adjust the plan as needed. Scientists say the difference between human and gorilla DNA is 2.8 percent.[2] It's not much, but it matters. Because of that 2.8 percent, humans have the ability to think—so, use it to your utmost potential. Superstar salespeople outthink others.

Recently, the media has featured a series of articles about the Human Genome Project, which is the effort to identify the human DNA map, cell by cell.[3] This evidence is significant considering it could move medicine from a reactive discipline into a proactive discipline. Scientists predict that if a baby were to be predisposed to a disease before birth, doctors would have the ability to prevent this by changing the cells. Although there are many ethical concerns to this debate, the bottom line is that this technology was discovered by the human intellect. This demonstrates a person's power to identify issues and problem-solve strategically. That's an important part of a salesperson's job. Think! And then, work with customers and coworkers to achieve the goal. Never underestimate your ability to excel and succeed. How good can you be?

Read this book diligently. The material can be implemented immediately because it's a selling workshop, designed to help you assess your strengths and areas of improvement. Complete the Superstar Selling Assessment, and then explore the details of each element throughout the rest of the book. There are complementary sales activity reflections to review and complete, so that you can quickly apply the ideas and skills discussed. For your encouragement, most of the concepts focus on staying positive while dealing with the challenges you face selling competitively in the marketplace. It's been said that if you increase your learning, you will increase your earning!

With 35 years of sales experience, we have worked with everyone— from the beginner to the best of the best. We have globally trained more than 250,000 salespeople in big and small, public and private companies. Superstar selling skills can catapult you into new levels of sales success, personal satisfaction, career achievement, and income potential. So, it's up to you now, isn't it? Begin today, so that you can be on your way to Superstar sales success.

How to Use This Book

Superstar salespeople take the right steps, which pays off in income, success, and happiness. Isn't it true that when you take shortcuts during the sales process, it often catches up with you later—causing problems that potentially reduce your ongoing sales and income? Would you agree with us that it is *right* to do the following?

▷ Be prepared to sell every day.

▷ Prospect positively daily.

▷ Build rapport with customers.

▷ Identify a need.

▷ Sell product benefits.

▷ Address concerns, positively.

▷ Close the sale.

▷ Follow up, follow up, and follow up.

By doing these tasks better and better, you help many more customers, sell much more, and earn a great living.

It's been said that success is simple: just do the right thing, in the right way, at the right time. However, in order to do what's right, you have to think about what's right. *Thought always precedes action.* Poor attitudes and negative thinking don't sell services or make you any money. In other words, to take the right actions, you have to have the right thoughts. That's the beginning of Superstar sales, and the key to making the Superstar selling process work for you.

William James once wrote, "The greatest discovery of my generation is that a human being can alter his life by altering his attitudes of mind."

You can, too! You have tremendous talent, skill, and potential. With the right thinking, you'll put all of your capabilities to use more consistently and passionately.

Believe!

In order to believe in positive results, you have to work at it. There are too many variables that affect our attitudes. We know them by heart: rejection, disappointment, frustration, illness, the news, complaining friends, and other elements. According to research, the average person thinks more than 10,000 thoughts each day, and 85 percent of those are negative.[1] You can't leave your attitude to chance. If you do, you're destined for failure or, worse yet, mediocrity.

How do you work at being positive? Start by thinking better about yourself. Believe you are the best version of yourself. We will review this in greater depth when we discuss emotional resiliency and peak performance. Next, review these two questions after every sale (especially after a lost sale):

▷ What did I do right?

▷ What can I do better or differently next time?

Often, salespeople get discouraged by a *no* and don't try again. Rather than doing this, when you get a *no,* think of how you feel when you get a *yes.* Review what you have done right, remind yourself that you're the best, and then take appropriate action. Contact another customer promptly, and then remember that the best time to make a sale is right after rejection. That's right! You build sales success through successful sales activity. Steve, a new sales manager, focused his team on this motto: excellent sales activity equals excellent sales results. It isn't surprising that his team is 50 percent or more above their sales goal. So, when you get a *no,* ask the two questions and then call another account.

Learn!

Do you have insurance? Auto? Health? People buy insurance for protection, don't they? In case of an illness or accident, insurance protects us from financial loss. As a salesperson, your most important personal assets are your skills, attitude, and experiences. Why not ensure that your assets are protected and that your ability to make money is established? Don't be content with the way things are. Keep learning, expand your comfort zones, and work at developing new skills, tools, and approaches.

Every year, as the baseball season begins, someone refuses to play because of a contract dispute. Consequently, the player misses part of training camp and, usually, starts the year poorly. In baseball and in sales, a lack of training yields poor results. Absorb all you can from your sales training and coaching sessions. Work on fundamentals by listening to CDs or podcasts, reading books, and attending sales seminars. Your thoughts will be more positive, your skills will improve, and your results will follow.

Act!

A goal is the most powerful motivational device known to man. It's a documented fact. We've seen goals inspire people to lose weight, finish a degree, achieve new results, sell a product, and make a lot of money. Are you attracted to any of these results? First set the goal, then regularly review your progress.

How can you offer more value to customers? Did you earn the money you wanted? What's your goal for the New Year? Take the time to make a plan and go for it—now! And, don't forget: excellent selling is excellent service.

Arlene Lenarz of Mary Kay wrote, "All the beautiful things that are going to happen in the future are the seeds of today. This is the year of your dreams. No matter what, if you want it badly enough, and you're willing to pay the price—your dream is possible. No dream is too lofty, no goal is too high." To succeed, you must be willing to do what others won't do. Implement these three sales ideas—believe, learn, and act to acquire the right thinking—and you'll become a Superstar. Here are four ways to believe in, learn from, and act on this book.

4 Ways to Benefit From Superstar Selling

First, we recommend you read the Contents, Introduction, and Days 1–4, which include the Superstar Selling Assessment, scoring, and definitions. Circle the topics of most interest or relevance to you in the Contents and read them next. All the basic sales skills are covered and sufficiently isolated in each chapter to give you tools and tips that will help you today.

Second, read the book at your leisure as you would any book. Contemplate the information and apply it as you go. Throughout the book you will be challenged with Sales Activity Reflections. These are applications to help you apply each concept. This is where the rubber meets the road. "Practice, drill, and rehearse" builds superstar results.

Third, use the book as a structured, 31-day improvement plan. Read one topic a day and act on the material. This way you will remain focused. As the saying goes, "How do you eat an elephant? One bite at a time." Within the 31 days you will begin to see changes in your sales effectiveness. It takes a few weeks to change habits anyway. With this process, you will be methodically working on good habits and reinforcing them daily.

Fourth, use the book as a resource when you are confronted with challenges or need a shot in the arm to achieve a breakthrough in sales. Again, we have written the book so the skills are broken down into bite-sized pieces that you can reference time and again.

Now, take the Superstar Selling Assessment and let your success journey begin.

Superstar Selling Assessment

Effective selling requires strong and varied skills. It is an unforgiving profession in which the true professionals will survive and win, and the pretenders will get pushed out of the mix unceremoniously. As a reference point, let me (Doug) tell you a little bit about my golfing skills. I grew up on a farm in southern Iowa and was a decent-sized duck, athletically speaking, in a very small pond. I don't mean to overstate my athletic career; it's just that my high school was very small, and we competed in a conference that was made up of very small schools. I enjoyed sports and got to play (as did my classmates) on most sports teams.

My community built a golf course when I was a sophomore in high school, so I thought it might be fun to learn how to play golf. I bought a basic set of clubs and went out a few times during the summers between high school and college. It's probably worth mentioning that I hit some golf balls in one of our pastures to "get the feel for it" before I went on the course. I didn't gain much skill in the game, but that didn't really matter to me because almost everyone else was playing at a similar level as I was. We were all friends, so it was good, low-pressure fun.

Fast-forward a few years—after I graduated from college, after I was married, and after I had begun my career. Some of my colleagues invited me to play golf one spring weekend in Delaware, home of my new job. I had the same old set of golf clubs and had not played golf since I roamed the community golf course in southern Iowa. I knew that I was going to have a miserable time unless I sharpened up my skills before I joined them at the club. In all honesty, it is probably only fair to say that I embarrassed myself anyway on that golf outing—and on many more golf outings through the years—but here is my point: I discovered, in conversation with one of my colleagues, that the University of Delaware had a small practice course that they used for research and education purposes, and where you could go and hit golf balls as poorly as you wanted without interfering with anybody else's game. In other words, it was the city version of a cow pasture in southern Iowa.

I spent several hours there practicing hitting my short irons. Then, I discovered that there was a small par-three course in my community as well, so that became my next step in my training to get ready to play golf with my colleagues. You can probably see where this is going, but I'll cut to the chase: Most of my practice centered on shots with my short irons. I became reasonably confident with my 9, 7, 5, and 3 irons. (I didn't have a full set of irons yet.) I had barely touched my driver and 3 wood. (I didn't have a full set of woods, either.) I also had minimal practice with my putter. And, I didn't own a sand wedge. If you are a golfer with even minimal experience, you know how poorly I played throughout that first spring and summer. You probably can also describe how I got into trouble, and the kinds of scores that I put up until I became more familiar with the game and gained some familiarity with the "tools." Decades have passed, and I enjoy the game, but am still not much more than a "weekend hacker." The game is unforgiving. It is dynamic, and you don't see the same challenge repeated during a round of golf. Your mistakes compound the difficulty of the game, and you can't fake it. Your true character and capability show up very quickly, and are apparent to every person who plays with you or watches you play.

There are many parallels with professional sales. In sales, your professional skill set must be broad and deep. Your ability to "read" and understand complex and ever-changing requirements and conditions are a bar you must clear to even be in the game. Your skill set, your character, your temperament, and your creativity are all on display continuously. Each decision you make and step you take has an impact on the possibility you'll succeed or that you'll fail. With all of this happening and more, your ability to maintain your composure and lead your customer and your company to success is pressing on you each minute of each day. It is no small thing to be a successful, professional salesperson.

As a sales professional, you have the opportunity and obligation to provide the highest quality products, services, and information to your customers. Notice that this assessment is customer-centered. Superstar salespeople are customer-focused, not self-focused. This requires a high degree of self-awareness, sales knowledge, and competence, and a good deal of organizational support and teamwork. The Superstar Selling Assessment is intended to help you self-assess and develop a plan to maximize your competence and your success. In order to build a solid foundation and to achieve better results, review what you do well and what you need to improve. Start by looking in the mirror.

In the tables on the following three pages, indicate the degree to which you see yourself as fully competent in the sales behavior described in each question. A candid assessment of yourself is needed. Use the following scale:

      1—Not at all

      2—To a very small degree

      3—To a small degree

      4—To some degree

      5—To a great degree

      6—To a very great degree

Then, add up the numbers in the "Total" line after each group of questions.

To what degree are you currently competent in:

A. Maintaining a Customer-Centered Focus		
1		Focusing entirely on the customer's world?
2		Confirming that the client understands your communication?
3		Reading the client's nonverbal cues?
4		Maintaining contact with customers?
5		Fostering long-term relationships?
6		Adapting behavior to cater to a client's reality?
7		Assessing the client's personality?
		TOTAL
B. Sales Planning and Preparation		
8		Developing prospective customers?
9		Accessing the decision-makers in client systems?
10		Monitoring the competition?
11		Establishing realistic goals?
12		Applying creativity to the selling process
13		Recording sales activities?
14		Engaging in time-and-territory planning?
15		Participating in sales-call planning?
16		Forecasting sales and profitability?
17		Adapting sales strategies to client information?
		TOTAL
C. Building Rapport With Customers		
18		Using the telephone to sell?
19		Communicating with a wide range of people?
20		Creating a positive first impression?
21		Making positive contact with the customer?
22		Building rapport?
23		Adapting your style in order to connect with the client?
24		Establishing a safe and constructive communication climate?
		TOTAL

D. Identifying Customer Needs		
25		Asking the client questions?
26		Listening intentionally?
27		Raising the client's awareness of unperceived needs?
28		Clarifying client problems?
29		Effectively distinguishing factual information from critical needs?
		TOTAL

E. Consulting With Clients		
30		Finding solutions to client problems?
31		Generating effective selling statements?
32		Demonstrating new products and processes?
33		Developing clear self-expression?
34		Maintaining active dialogue in sales presentations?
35		Conducting yourself persuasively?
36		Delivering presentations to a group audience?
37		Using audiovisual aids (e.g., computer technology) to sell?
38		Simplifying technical presentations?
39		Identifying the benefits to the client?
40		Using sales support (e.g., statistics, exhibits)?
		TOTAL

F. Addressing Client Concerns		
41		Asking for feedback on proposed solutions?
42		Expressing empathy for others?
43		Managing resistance from the client?
44		Addressing interpersonal conflict?
45		Repairing damaged sales relationships?
		TOTAL

G. Finalizing the Agreement		
46		Closing by asking for the business?
47		Securing the client's commitments?
48		Demonstrating assertiveness during negotiations?
	TOTAL	
H. Follow-Up and Follow-Through		
49		Using the telephone to maintain sales relationships?
50		Re-establishing dormant account relationships?
51		Sending written correspondence to customers?
52		Sending written correspondence within your company?
53		Keeping appropriate records?
54		Increasing the focus on existing accounts?
	TOTAL	
I. Leveraging Team and Organizational Support		
55		Functioning as a team member in selling?
56		Relating effectively to sales-support personnel?
57		Taking quick action in critical situations?
	TOTAL	
J. Emotional Resiliency and Peak Performance		
58		Learning your company's products and services in depth?
59		Staying informed about your company's products and services?
60		Handling rejection appropriately?
61		Evaluating personal sales-call performances?
	TOTAL	

Try not to become a man of success but rather to become a man of value.

—Albert Einstein

Superstar Sales Definitions and Assessment Scoring

Sales professionals can be successful in a number of different ways. One may be particularly strong at establishing new account relationships. Another may be most effective at building trusting relationships and carefully understanding the needs and objectives of customers. And many others are highly knowledgeable about their products and services. Yet, research suggests that effective salespeople excel in several key areas. Superstar selling requires versatility, a strong skill set, and an unwavering commitment to customer-centered activity. Here are the 10 critical competencies that will spark success in your sales world.

Customer-Centered Activity: approaching the sales relationship and focusing entirely on the customer's needs, wants, and expectations. A commitment to adjust behavior accordingly, communicate effectively, act ethically, read nonverbal cues, help customers achieve their goals, cater to the client's style and personality, and confirm that communication is properly understood during the entire buying process.

Effective Sales-Call Planning: determining your position in the sales relationship, planning your sales activity sequence appropriately, generating profitable and mutually beneficial outcomes for you and your customers, managing your time and resources in ways that maximize their value, building effective business results for your customers, working collaboratively, and coordinating internal resources. Other skills include time-and-territory planning, individual sales-call planning, and annual strategic business planning.

Building Customer Rapport: establishing rapport, making positive impressions, building trust, listening intently, creating a safe and constructive communication climate, building relationships with key decision-influencers, and connecting with your customers by using all communication tools at your disposal.

Identifying Customer Needs: planning and executing discussions and meetings that enable you and your client to think through personal and professional needs in a way that results in a mutual realization of the best product or service solution that addresses the client's unmet and undefined needs. Asking appropriate questions, listening carefully, setting aside predetermined thoughts and solutions, learning, and raising the client's awareness of overlooked needs.

Consulting With Clients: developing solutions to client problems, generating effective selling statements, demonstrating new products and processes, expressing yourself clearly, maintaining active dialogue in presentations, acting in a persuasive manner, presenting effectively to group audiences, using sales support effectively, and simplifying technical presentations.

Addressing Customer Concerns: requesting feedback on your proposed solutions, expressing empathy for others, managing client resistance, dealing with interpersonal conflict, and repairing broken sales relationships. This competency involves skillfully applying the ability to generate dialogue and mutual involvement in the sales process with the customer, while competently working with the customer when she is frustrated, angry, or opposed to your solution.

Finalizing Agreement: directing all sales activity toward specific outcomes. This competency also involves encouraging the customer to commit to using you and your products, demonstrating assertiveness during negotiations, asking for the business, and securing client commitments.

Follow-Up and Follow-Through: maintaining sales relationships by using the telephone, sending appropriate and relevant correspondence to customers, reestablishing dormant account relationships, taking action, coordinating activities and outcomes within your company, keeping appropriate records, and increasing the focus on existing accounts.

Leveraging Team and Organizational Support: functioning as an external/internal team member, effectively relating to sales-support personnel, taking prompt action during critical situations, and aligning activities to customer commitments and expectations.

Emotional Resiliency and Peak Performance: maintaining proper life balance by handling rejection and stress appropriately, evaluating personal sales-call performance, and committing to ongoing learning and development.

To summarize, outstanding sales professionals are consistently growing in each of these 10 competencies. You don't simply master one and then take it for granted. You keep polishing your skills and expanding your knowledge. As the old adage goes, life is a journey, not a destination. Establishing excellence in sales is a process that includes periodically taking inventory of your strengths and areas of improvement, and then taking action. We will cover each of these areas as they relate to the Superstar selling model. To begin, you need two things:

1. A strong awareness of your abilities in each of these competencies.
2. A plan to excel.

Everyone lives by selling something.

—Robert Louis

Superstar Selling Assessment Score Sheet

Transfer your scores from the Superstar Selling Assessment in Day 1 to the appropriate spaces here.

Items	Competency	Score
1–7	Customer-Centered: The ability to focus on the customer's world and avoid preoccupation with your own needs.	
8–17	Sales Planning: The degree to which you are able to orchestrate and execute an effective, results-producing plan.	
18–24	Building Customer Rapport: The ability to establish rapport with customers, even when they are out of sync with your preferred style.	
25–29	Identifying Customer Needs: The ability to ask the right questions to diagnose customer needs and create a mutual understanding of client priorities.	
30–40	Consulting with Clients: The ability to engage your clients in a compelling and results-producing presentation that highlights your solutions to the client's needs.	
41–45	Addressing Customer Concerns: Effectively generating feedback and constructively working with client objections, frustrations, and disagreements.	
46–48	Finalizing Agreement: The ability to encourage the client to commit to and follow through with mutual action on business agreements.	
49–54	Follow-Up and Follow-Through: The ability to recognize follow-up opportunities, and the initiative to take steps toward building long-term relationships.	
55–57	Leveraging Team and Organizational Support: Effectively orchestrating appropriate resources to generate customer results.	
58–61	Emotional Resiliency and Peak Performance: Personally taking steps to manage individual learning and mastery as a professional.	

Superstar Assessment Interpretation

Sales Competency	Score	✓
Customer-Centered: The ability to focus on the customer's world and avoid preoccupation with your own needs.	35–42 21–34 7–20	Highly capable Development recommended Needs immediate work
Sales Planning: The degree to which you are able to orchestrate and execute an effective, results-producing plan.	50–60 30–49 10–29	Highly capable Development recommended Needs immediate work
Building Customer Rapport: The ability to establish rapport with customers, even when they are out of sync with your preferred style.	35–42 21–34 7–20	Highly capable Development recommended Needs immediate work
Identifying Customer Needs: The ability to ask the right questions to diagnose customer needs and create a mutual understanding of priorities.	25–30 15–24 5–14	Highly capable Development recommended Needs immediate work
Consulting With Customers: The ability to engage customers in a compelling presentation that highlights your solutions to their needs.	56–66 23–55 11–22	Highly capable Development recommended Needs immediate work
Addressing Client Concerns: Effectively generating feedback and constructively working with client objections and frustrations.	25–30 15–24 5–14	Highly capable Development recommended Needs immediate work
Finalizing Agreement: The ability to encourage the client to commit to and follow through with mutual action on business agreements.	15–18 9–14 3–8	Highly capable Development recommended Needs immediate work

Sales Competency	Score	✓
Follow-Up and Follow-Through: The ability to recognize follow-up opportunities and take steps to build long-term relationships.	30–36 18–29 6–17	Highly capable Development recommended Needs immediate work
Leveraging Team and Organizational Support: Effectively orchestrating appropriate resources to generate customer results.	15–18 9–14 3–8	Highly capable Development recommended Needs immediate work
Emotional Resiliency and Peak Performance: Taking steps to manage personal mastery.	20–24 12–19 4–11	Highly capable Development recommended Needs immediate work

SuperStar Selling Assessment Circumplex

Scoring Instructions

1. Plot your scores on the blank circumplex below by placing your numerical rating on the numbered scale within each dimension. Shade each dimension of your circumplex to create a graphic representation of your scores.

2. Compare your scoring profile (image) to those presented below.

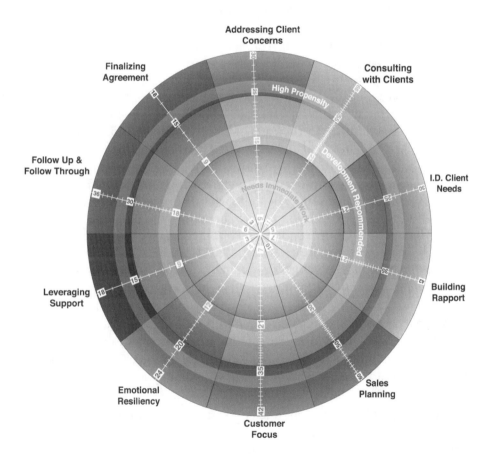

Profile Review

The following descriptions provide a series of profiles based on some common archetypal sales profiles. The data are presented on a circumplex, a tool deigned to highlight interpersonal data in three ways that we find useful for developmental purposes:

1. Your score for each individual dimension of sales effectiveness is presented on **a numerical scale that numerically and graphically provides perspective on the relative strength of that dimension.** Lower on the scale indicates more need for development, and higher on the scale represents a higher level of skill.

2. **The interplay between the competencies also has an impact on the effect of your sales approach.** The old phrase "like a hammer in search of a nail" highlights the reality that many of us rely so much on a skill or set of skills that we overuse or misuse those skills in a way that makes us less effective in a somewhat-predictable manner. This interplay and its result on your sales approach can be identified by asking: What is the effect of a high level of skill and utilization here, combined with less skill and use of this (particular) skill?

3. The overall image or **shape of our skills (via the circumplex) will provide a glimpse of your total development opportunity** in a way that is not available simply by looking at the numerical representation. For example: Are you well-rounded in your competency set, or does your circumplex appear to be "jagged," meaning there are highs and lows to your overall approach? Are most of your skills in the "highly capable" range, or are many or most in the "development recommended" or "development needed" range?

Review the scoring profiles and compare your scoring patterns to the archetypal descriptions provided along with each circumplex. It is not possible to describe every scoring image that might occur, so you may find a close approximation to yours or you may have to look for pattern similarities and read the description to best formulate your own competency description.

Note: This tool is presented as a training aid, and not as an "assessment." By this, we mean that your scores are self reported and represent your viewpoint at a point in time. The intention here is to help you identify current strengths and development opportunities. Just as you can become a better golfer by identifying specific areas of your game for focused improvement and practice, so you can improve as a sales professional by choosing your areas of focus and going to work.

The Visitor

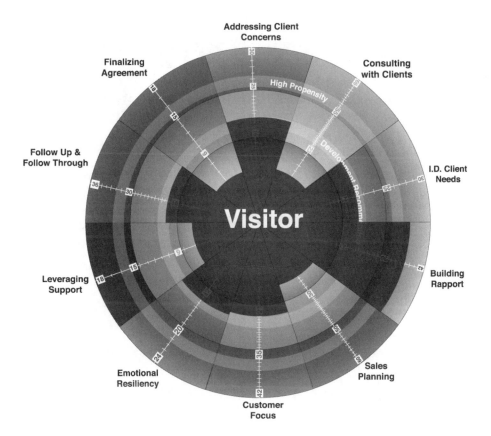

The visitor profile is represented by particularly high scores in building (and maintaining) rapport. The visitor's scores are often mid-range to high in follow-up and follow-through. The visitor's scores indicate that the relationship is of paramount importance, and the business development elements of the selling relationship receive far less effort and attention. Therefore, finalizing agreement scores are often low, as are scores in consulting with clients, the actual solution-generation portion of the sales process. Sales planning scores are relatively low, and customer focus is often in the mid-range because, although the salesperson focuses on the customer, most of the focus is centered on building and maintaining the relationship, with little or no focus on getting into the customer's viewpoint and generating strong business-producing solutions.

The Presenter

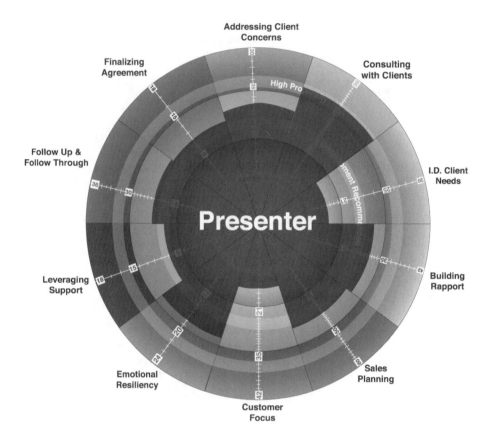

This archetype presents high scores on consulting with clients, and low- to mid-range scores on building and maintaining rapport and on follow-up and follow-through. They also often have lower scores on customer focus and low to mid-range on sales planning. Sales professionals with this profile place high value on understanding products and their features. They work very hard on making strong and forceful presentations to the customer. What gets left out in the process, however, is the connection to the customer's personal and business needs. As a result, the balance is lost between the business presentation and the business needs the solution should relate to. Presenters are often quite frustrated because they're certain that they present the best picture of the company and its products, and they can't understand why the customer isn't buying.

The Interrogator

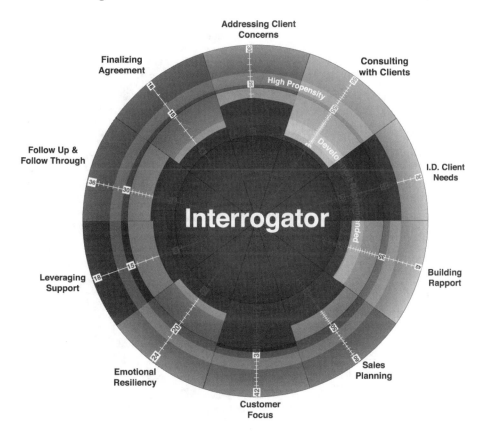

The interrogator puts a great deal of emphasis on the questioning (investigative) aspects of the sales relationship. Exploring customer needs and understanding the business conditions that created them put the interrogator in position to present a solution that meets the customer's needs. Scores in identifying client needs have a tendency to be high on the circumplex. The presentation side (consulting with clients) will not be scored as high. There is always more information to gather and understand, and as a result, this profile can feel like the old metaphor "ready, aim, aim, aim, aim…." The customer may ultimately feel as though they have been turned inside out and examined, but there is never a solution or resolution. The interrogator may believe that he is building strong rapport, not realizing that the impact of his questioning can be to reduce trust and create distance in the relationship with the customer.

The Closer

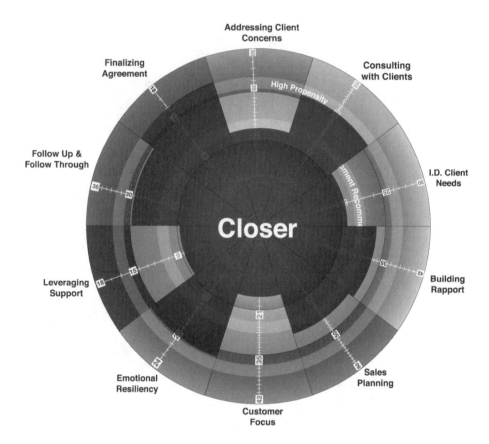

The closer typically has strong skills and an orientation to presenting, which result in high scores on consulting with clients because that is the most direct pathway to finalizing agreements. A closer also works hard on follow-up and follow-through because she is a continuation of the "push" for the final sale (close). The scores on emotional resiliency will often be in the mid-range to higher because the results focus often carries with it some blindness to the pull back or move away that their pushiness generates in customers. The closer will often have lower scores on identifying client needs. And the closer's needs identification process is often shallower and more representative of finding a fit with her product than it is with generating a customer solution that provides value for the customer.

Misplaced Loyalty

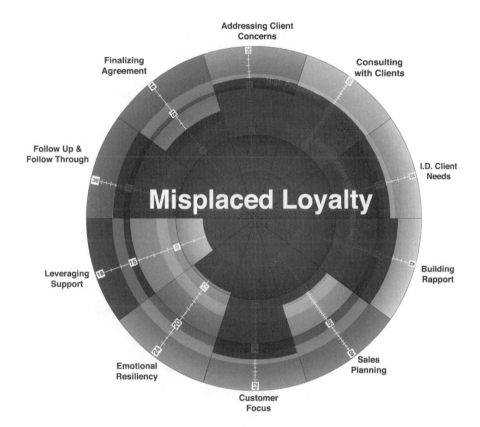

The misplaced loyalty archetype shows up with high scores in customer focus and identifying customer needs. He typically has a high degree of understanding of the customer and his needs, and how the customer's business problems can be resolved. The counterbalancing competency here is typically a low score in leveraging business resources and support to address customer needs. This sales professional commonly relates so strongly to his customer's issues and becomes so frustrated with his inability to get the needed support for his own organization that he relates more to his customers than his own organization. This misplaced loyalty puts him out of position in the customer relationship and undermines his impact.

The Planner

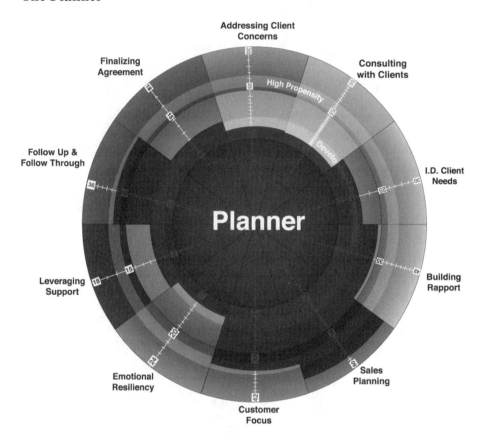

A sales professional who fits the profile of a planner scores high in sales planning, customer focus, and follow-up and follow-through. The strong point about a planner is that she has her act together when she shows up with her customer. She has a strong agenda and direction, and she knows exactly what she wants to do with the customer. The risk is that she often puts a lot of emphasis on developing her plans, but the execution of her plans may be lacking. Her efforts to build rapport, consult with her clients, finalize agreements, and leverage support may all be relatively low. Her emotional resilience and the tie-in between her focus on planning and the low tendency toward execution, result in a high degree of frustration, because the results never seem to follow the image that is present in the planner's mind.

Average

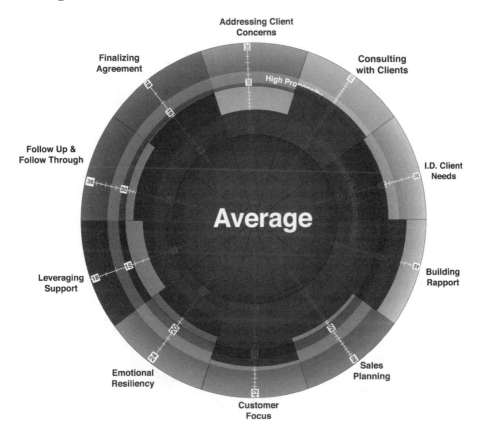

The average sales performer's scores are represented by scores that fall into the high "development recommended" and/or low-high propensity range across the board. It is fairly common for the core sales skills (building rapport, identifying customer needs, presenting, and closing) to be pretty strong. Often, his scores (and performance) aren't so high in the sales planning that will be needed to position him well within the client's company. There may be some areas where his scores (and relative strengths) may be higher or lower, but overall the scores are just average. There is often a high degree of potential for growth and development if the average sales professional will systematically identify potential areas for focus and work to lift his skills and efforts.

The Expert

An expert (Superstar) is represented by high scores in all competency areas, depicting a well-rounded, highly capable, and (most likely) high-performing sales professional. A sales professional with scores this high across all dimensions of our sales model is a standout in performance. Her capability and value are easily recognized by sales management, and her customers see her as a valuable contributor to her (customer) business. This is absolutely the model of excellence that we are seeking to reproduce throughout sales organizations.

Sales Activity Reflection: Action-Planning Guide

Instructions: You'll recall that earlier we discussed the four steps to benefit from Superstar selling. This Sales Activity Reflection is the first structured opportunity for you to begin your action-planning for improvement. This one is also particularly important because it gives you a very real opportunity to stop and take a look in the mirror. This assessment gives you a comprehensive look at your sales competency and a very real opportunity to choose your initial steps to become the most effective sales professional you can be. There aren't very many questions, but they present a great opportunity for you to start off on a productive journey. Give them your best thought and effort.

1. After reviewing your circumplex and comparing it to the archetypes presented, does your scoring profile appear to share similarities with any of them? In what ways does your selling approach mirror any of the archetypes presented?

2. List two or three strengths based on your inventory.

3. Choose two or three that would give you the biggest "bang for the buck" if you improved.

4. What benefit is there for you if you improve in these areas?

5.What efforts have you made in the past? What worked?

6. What resources are available to support you in these
   developmental areas?

7. What are your intended first steps?

8. Who needs to know about your plan?

9. How will you recruit others to help you?

Warning: Pessimism Is Hazardous to Your Health!

A 25-year study at the world-renowned Mayo Clinic determined that pessimism is hazardous to your health. To identify optimism and pessimism tendencies, the Mayo Clinic distributed a personality test to hundreds of participants. The results proved that, on average, pessimistic people die 19 percent earlier than optimistic individuals; in other words, optimistic people live 13–14 *years* longer, suffer less illness, and experience a better quality of life.[1] Who wouldn't be happy to hear these results?

Some people like to complain, others like to criticize everything, and then there are a few who have bad news by the hour. These attitudes destroy sales, decrease income opportunities, and, according to the Mayo Clinic, diminish life expectancy.

Optimism and positive attitudes make everything better, especially in sales. It all begins with your goals—what do you really want in life? We recently asked this question of Superstar salespeople. Their responses fit into the following categories:

•Health/wellness.	•Happiness.
•Self-satisfaction.	•Enjoyment.
•Travel.	•Quality family time.
•Recognition.	•Material things.
•Security.	•Money.
•Success.	•Fun.

Where do your responses fit? These desires are the true motivators in life. It's not about the contests, products, or quotas you get from your company. For any person, the clearer you are about what you want, the more specific your goals, and the sooner you take action, the faster you'll make these dreams a reality. *We still live in a land of opportunity.* As William Clement Stone said, "Whatever the mind of man can conceive and believe, it can achieve!"

Why not get positive and optimistic today? This takes work, too. Why not take action and stay focused on the Superstar selling strategies? Sales winners do it. You're worth it, aren't you? It comes down to accountability, right? It's been said, "If it is to be, it's up to me!" Nobody can do it for you. You have to take action and make something happen for yourself. Do it for your own reasons. Do it for yourself and your family. Remember to stay positive!

Again, use the Sales Activity Reflections throughout the book as opportunities to grow, learn, and develop you capabilities. If you like to write things or think them through, use them as a tool to train yourself to win. May the best of success be yours!

> *Learn from each situation how to do it better the next time.*
>
> —Tom Hopkins

Sales Activity Reflection: Opportunity for Change

If pessimism is this bad for you, we can't just rush right past this point! Very rarely is pessimism something we're intentionally or thoughtfully choosing; however, once it becomes our way of living, it can become so innate that changing our ways can feel as though we're going against the wind.

So, if you're a pessimistic person, take some time to make a plan on how you're going to head in the direction of change. Thinking, being, and living positively is possible, even if you're living pessimistically now. Awareness is the first step toward change. So let's start there.

1. After reading the Mayo Clinic health study results, how did you feel?

2. On a scale of 1–10 (1 = very pessimistic; 10 = very optimistic), how would you rate yourself currently? Why do you give yourself this rating?

3. As you reflect on your life, has that number changed over time? What's responsible for the change that's taken place?

4. Who are the three most positive people you know? How does being around them make you feel?

5. How do you want to make those around you feel?

6. What are three things you want to start doing to become more positive?

If you're already an optimistic person, great! Keep making positive living a priority!

The Superstar Selling Process

To be the best, you have to be willing to do what others are unwilling to do. You have to be willing to learn what others don't know. The old adage that claims winning isn't everything is misleading; sales professionals of all industries know that although winning isn't everything, the will to prepare to win *is*. Bert Jones, a Superstar salesperson, understood this concept when he claimed, "You can't *teach* others how to sell. You can only teach them *how to learn* how to sell." Our approach in this book is similar to that belief; the Superstar selling process is geared toward one customer and one sales call at a time.

How good can you really be? Are you willing to do the preparation required to achieve what you want? We have seen sales professionals develop the competencies and apply the Superstar selling model in ways that increase their sales from 30 to 52 percent—some even to 124 percent! Most continue to improve for another three to five years, and then maintain a high level of excellence. Remember, an increase in sales means an increase in income!

Why can't you achieve this same level of success? You can! It doesn't matter if you are a beginner or a sales veteran. Sometimes, veterans have created so many ingrained habits over the years that they have even more to learn and relearn. The good news is that positive change can happen, and, in most cases, it can happen quickly! Why? Because you can start increasing sales using proven and practical approaches now!

Review the Superstar Selling Model on page 48. Notice how it relates to the assessment. Three parts aren't on the model, but they do circumvent each step:

▷ Customer-centered.

▷ Leveraging team and organizational support.

▷ Emotional resiliency and peak performance.

We need to align our approach with the customer's position in the purchasing process if we hope to be successful. We will talk more about that later. For now, let's dig into the key stages of the Superstar selling process.

> *Excellent selling is excellent service, and excellent service is excellent selling!*
>
> —Rick Conlow

The Superstar Selling Process

Too many sales professionals complain because they can only focus on how bad it is, and they forget that they are responsible for the situation they have created. Others let their sales activity get them down. Sales has built-in rejection and negativity if you let it get to you. Did you ever have a bad day? You missed a few sales or a few deals turned out differently than you had hoped. The key is how you handle it. Do you ask, *What did I do wrong?* Or, do you ask, *What can I learn?* This defines the difference between pessimism or optimism. Why not take action and stay focused on the Superstar selling strategies? Sales winners do it. You're worth it, aren't you? It comes down to accountability, right?

It's been said, "If it is to be, it's up to me!" Nobody can do it for you. You have to take action and make something happen for yourself. Do it for your own reasons. Do it for yourself and your family. Remember to stay positive! Use these reflection points as an opportunity to grow, learn, and develop you capabilities. May the best of success be yours!

> *I have never worked a day in my life without selling.*
> *If I believe in something, I sell it, and I sell it hard.*
>
> —Estée Lauder

Sales Activity Reflection: Starting Point

Now that you have taken the Superstar Selling Assessment, learned about the various sales dimensions, and committed to becoming a Superstar sales professional, it's time for a moment of self-reflection before we dig in to the details of each sales competency.

We recently read a story of a high school athlete who set a state record of scoring more than 4,300 points in his career. He was averaging 42.1 points his senior year. He made the varsity team as an eighth grader. Besides basketball practice and camps, he practiced shooting more than 400 shots every day.[1] We emphasize again that you use these reflection points as a powerful guide—practice time—to help you become a more successful salesperson, if not a sales Superstar.

1. What brought you to this book? What motivated you to start focusing on your selling skills?

2. What long-term selling goals do you have that you want to use these skills to achieve?

3. What's in it for you to become a Superstar sales professional?

4. When you read the question, "How good can you be?" what answers came to mind? How good can you be? (Dream big and stay positively focused.)

5. What is the one thing you want to remind yourself of throughout this Superstar selling journey?

Strategic Sales Planning and Preparation

When you think about your job as a sales professional, how much of your time is spent strategically planning for sales and generating activity that's designed to sell? Though there is always a certain amount of market planning and strategic effort required during the product-development launch stage, how much planning time is put into customer interactions? We have learned that whatever time is currently designated to planning, it isn't enough, mainly because everyone is so busy with this, that, and the other thing. Superstars plan well, without overdoing it, and they make more sales.

We believe in strategic sales planning and preparation. (Whether you are in business to business selling or consumer selling this is crucial to your success story.) In some ways, strategic sales planning is like chess; we must think and plan several steps ahead. We want to act with a more comprehensive understanding of each player's position. And we want our efforts to be governed by the customer's business, personal needs, and goals while we take into account our competitor's activities and our own desired outcomes. Finally, we must consider selling something today, while at the same time strategically planning for the long term, so that we anticipate business changes that evolve from customer activities.

We will consider a number of tools here. Each is intended to give us a "lens" to look through when planning our sales activity. We don't know very many sales professionals who can afford to waste time randomly calling on accounts and trying the same approach over and over. It makes a great deal more sense to use your planning time and tools to look at each account or prospective account critically, and to make decisions about where to use your time most productively and how to use your skills to win the most business available.

1. The **Sales Potential Matrix** helps us determine the difference between a *valued customer* and an *expandable customer.* This matrix allows us to consider the criteria that can be used to help us identify our accounts with the most growth potential. The key operating principle is to utilize our scarce resources to our advantage. One of the primary resources is the potential customer pool at our disposal. To determine which accounts have the most potential, we suggest using the Sales Potential Matrix to evaluate the business within each of our current accounts. Continued success requires an appropriate mix of customers, balanced between the potential risk and return.

2. **Prospecting for Profit** is an A-B-C method for finding and calling on new accounts. Most companies today provide qualified prospect lists for their reps. They use Dun and Bradstreet or Data.com for this. What you need to do is create a game plan to call on those accounts. Cold calling is tough. You have to warm them up and then follow a prioritized campaign strategy.

3. To ensure that we understand how decisions are made, we will explore the various **buyer roles and decision styles** within an organization. Once we are aware of these roles, we are much more likely to tailor our selling activities according to the customer's buying process.

4. The **Sales Relationship Map** allows us to consider our position within each account, which helps us adjust our selling activity in ways that allow us to advance within an account. Our position on the map gives us guidance as to how to pursue additional business, so that we can progress on the map.

5. The **SWOT Analysis** reviews the organization from a practical perspective, using the identification of its strengths, weaknesses, opportunities, and threats. This allows us to focus on high-priority, high-payoff opportunities to develop our solution. We will review and develop our skills to determine our *value proposition,* which includes the resources, tools, skills,

services, and products that our company can provide that differentiate our offer from the competition and add value to our proposed solution. We will also evaluate the competitors' activity to determine how to best counter or overcome their strategies. Combining these tools gives us indicators and diagnostics that we can use to identify our position in the competitive playing field. With this knowledge and awareness, we can plan our activities more effectively and utilize our resources to achieve our strategic objectives.

Character cannot be developed in ease and quiet. Only through experience of trial and suffering can the soul be strengthened, ambition inspired, and success achieved.

—Helen Keller

Sales Activity Reflection: Your Planning Personality

Before we move into the Market Potential Matrix, let's stop, so that you can assess your planning personality. Planning is one way of preparing; it's not the only way, but we believe it's an essential part of the preparation equation.

Alan Lakein, an author and time-management expert, says in *How to Get Control of Your Time and Your Life*, "Failing to plan is planning to fail." Now, although luck is sometimes in your favor, if you want to increase your odds for consistent success, start planning! Take this quick, five-question quiz to determine your planning personality. Rate yourself on a scale of 1–5 depending on how often you do the following.

5 = Almost Always

4 = Often

3 = Occasionally

2 = Seldom

1 = Almost Never

1. If you spend a total of 10 hours on one customer, two hours (or more) of that time are committed to planning and preparing for the call.

| 1 | 2 | 3 | 4 | 5 |

2. If you have a prior personal relationship with a sales client, preparing is less of a priority because you already know what you need to know about that client.

| 1 | 2 | 3 | 4 | 5 |

3. You feel very unprepared when you don't thoroughly research the customer sales and prepare your sales call thoroughly.

| 1 | 2 | 3 | 4 | 5 |

4. If you are really busy and have been experiencing a lot of sales success, the easiest place to cut back, in order to save time, is the planning stage.

| 1 | 2 | 3 | 4 | 5 |

5. You invest more time understanding your client than you spend face-to-face with your client.

| 1 | 2 | 3 | 4 | 5 |

There are no right answers. In our opinion, however, the higher the score on questions 1, 3, and 5, the better; and on questions 2 and 4, the lower the better.

The Sales Potential Matrix and Prospecting for Profit

To win more business and make more money, you need to sell more to current customers and gain business from the best potential new prospects. In this chapter we will look at the Sales Potential Matrix and Prospecting for Profit.

Sales Potential Matrix

Before we even begin to contact current customers, an important strategy question must be asked: Where is the best opportunity? Where are the best sales targets (potential customers) to invest our time? There is a difference between *valued customers* and *expandable customers*. Certainly, every customer that has the potential to use our products is a valued customer relationship that we want to foster. But, valuing a customer and protecting a customer from competitors require different activities, in order to build business and to expand sales. Making this distinction is important for us to do.

Using the matrix is one way we can look at each current customer through two dimensions:

1. First, we must review the amount of business we own, as a percentage of all of the potential business (that we know of). For example, if we sold 20 products a month to a customer that occupied 50 percent or more of that area's sales activity, we would know we own a high percentage of activity in that area. Alternatively, if we sold one product to one account per week, we would know we own a small percentage of that business.

2. The other dimension considers account growth potential. Typically, there are two ways an account can grow. The first is to expand our market potential by finding more new customers than we have at a given point. Do this by conducting research, contacting marketing companies, using industry associations, purchasing mailing lists, or hiring a consultant. The second is to win more share of the business we have. We can do this by upgrading our product advantage to current customers to ensure our company products have a larger share of their business. In the matrix, the vertical axis is occupied by the amount of business owned, whereas the growth potential is on the horizontal axis. This allows us to plot four distinct matrix positions:

Flatliner: If we own a small percentage of an account's business and there's little growth potential, then there is little opportunity for our company to grow. Customers in this quadrant are unwilling to consider buying more of our products as a percentage of their overall sales. This category is not a priority; it's more about maintaining the minimal sales they are contributing, without wasting too much of our time on them.

Valued: If we own a high percentage of an account's business, but there's little growth potential, we want to protect that account and take advantage of ongoing profitability that's available to us. Because the potential is minimal, we don't want to over-invest, but we do want to provide what's appropriate to allow the account to continue using our products. We want to protect the business that's there, maintain the relationship, and preserve the account, so that competitors don't impede on our position.

High Potential: When we own a small amount of an account's existing business but there's potential for growth, our strategic goal should be to build upon the existing potential. Increasing our market share or capturing market share from our competitors may generate this growth. This category is worth our time and attention. Customers with high potential for increased purchase of our products and services deserve a high level of generative effort and activity.

Expandable: Another high-potential customer includes the *expandable* customer. We already own a high percentage of this customer's business, and there's potential for future growth, so this customer deserves our best, most persistent efforts.

Sales Potential Matrix

Note: The time investment choices are presented as examples only.

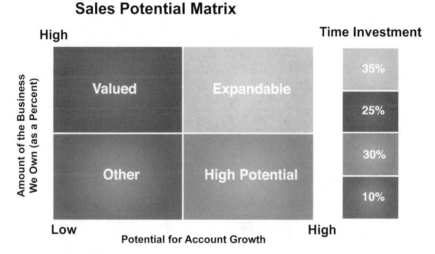

- Low presence/low potential: Don't invest time. (Kill it)
- Low presence/high potential: Build and execute strategy to win. (Build it)
- High presence/low potential: Milk and protect it. (Insulate it)
- High presence/high potential: Expandable. (Grow it and grow with it)

Sales Activity Reflection: Current Customers

Determine where you are spending most of your time and effort right now. Use the following chart to identify where five of your accounts fall on the Sales Potential Matrix, and then determine the appropriate action based on your analysis. In the other sales activities, use the highest-priority accounts to apply the sales skills that are discussed.

Account	Position	Action
1.		
2.		
3.		
4.		
5.		

Prospecting for Profit

As you prospect for profit, keep the following quote in mind:

> *It's not what you want to sell when you want to sell it that matters today. It's what the customer wants to buy when the customer wants it that counts.*

—John Graham

In our experience, the average salesperson spends 75 percent of his or her time on something other than face-to-face customer interactions. By increasing your customer time to consume more of your time or at least 50 percent of your time, you will increase your contacts, appointments, sales, and income.

Although numbers matter in terms of how much money you make, it's not necessarily a numbers game in prospecting. It's all about quality. Quality leads plus a quality effort equals more sales and more cash.

Cold calling today is a tough sale. People are so busy and tired of fast-talking salespeople calling them on the phone. Customers distrust cold-calling salespeople. For example, how much would you trust a Wall Street broker who calls you out of the blue and wants you to invest only $25,000 today? Many companies keep encouraging this kind of approach. Cold calling:

▷ Is a rude interruption to the customer.

▷ Paints you as a desperate product peddler.

▷ Wastes time on many unqualified leads to find a few qualified ones.

▷ Is asking someone to marry you on the first date; you come across as pushy and distrustful.

▷ Is disliked by most salespeople because of the high rejection rate.

We have found you need to do four things to improve results:

1. Clarify the benefits you have over your competition and target a market that needs them.

2. Create a prospecting for profit campaign to "warm up" or qualify your opportunities who want to buy.

3. Collate your information into a customer management system to track results.

4. Commit to a consistent effort.

Clarify Your Benefits: Target a Market

This may be simplistic to suggest, but it is powerful in practice. There are three key questions you need to answer:

1. Why should a customer trust you?

2. What makes you better or different?

3. Why should a customer buy from you?

There are many retailers that sell clothing (Wal-Mart, Target, Kohl's, JC Penney, Sears, Macy's, and Nordstrom, to name a few). Each retailer has had to carefully craft a strategy for its business. For example, Wal-Mart is all about the lowest price. Nordstrom has the best service. Customers know what to expect when they shop at these stores. Those retailers who have a hard time differentiating themselves end up in trouble in the marketplace.

Now think about you. What is it that will make a customer want to work with you? It usually will involve an edge in price, product (technology), place (company reputation), or people (your experience or reputation).

Once you know this, you need to establish a list of customers. Think of current customers and others in your industry like them. If your company doesn't feed you leads, as mentioned previously, with a little online research you can find services that provide lists and/or research your accounts for you. How many prospects do you need?

▷ Determine the income you want. (Let's say $75,000.)

▷ Determine the average sale and commission earned. (Let's say your average sale is $10,000 and the average commission is $2,500 per sale.)

▷ Divide the two (income by commission) in order to calculate the number of sales you need. ($75,000/$2,500 = 30 sales)

▷ Determine the average closing rate on proposals presentations (or buying customer contacts, depending on the type of sales you are in) to determine how many you need to make to reach the number of closed sales you need. (Let's say your closing rate is 33%. So it takes three proposals to get one sale. So you need 30 × 3 or 90 proposals to reach your income goal.)

▷ Identify the number of prospects that it takes to have a proposal presentation. (Let's say it takes 3 prospects to get to one proposal. So you need 90 × 3 or 270 prospects to get to your goal.

You can always improve these numbers by doing a better job of qualifying prospects, increasing your sales average, or improving your closing rate. Each of these is interrelated.

Finally, identify which of your prospects are most like your valued accounts and need the benefits you provide, which prospects are next in line, and which prospects are least desirable but have potential. Now, you'll need to decide how you will get in front of them.

Create a Prospecting for Profit Campaign

To warm up your qualified customers you need to gain their awareness and begin to build their trust. What you want is a series of messages directed to the customer through direct mail, e-mail, and a follow-up phone call.

Send a direct mail letter with a flyer that outlines your benefits. It's easy to create such letters and flyers with today's word-processing capabilities. Check with your marketing department (if you have one) for flyers already in the queue or to get help on this.

E-mail campaigns through Constant Contact, Infusionsoft, or others like them are good ways to build and execute a campaign to attract customers who are highly qualified. Through Windows you can do a mail merge. This isn't as robust as some of the other options, but it is cheaper. A campaign is usually a series of 10–20 e-mails over a couple of weeks promoting a beneficial offer. Always include a call to action. You can also generate newsletters in a similar way. Many companies are beginning processes like this. Because this kind of customer interaction is so easy and affordable, most salespeople can start their own initiatives, as well.

Finally, you call the account. See Day 11: Rapport Building for a sample letter and phone script. Most of the time your goal is to get an appointment. Your direct mail and e-mail campaigns have created awareness of you and your benefits. There are two schools of thought on the phone calls for appointments. Either schedule your own appointments or get an assistant to call and schedule an appointment for you. We have found that the higher the complexity of the sale and the more important the relationship, the more critical it is for you to make your own calls. Try both and see what works the best for you.

Collate Your Information: Track Results

It's hard to manage it if you don't measure it. Many tools are available: ACT software, Goldmine software, or online systems such as Saleforce .com. Most forward-looking companies have some sort of an approach for customer relationship management (CRM). Maximize your CRM to keep track of your sales activity. You can't control the market or even customer behavior, but you can control your sales activity. If your company doesn't have a system, get one of your own. Search online and compare price and functionality. Also, if you don't measure it, it doesn't get done with excellence.

Commit to a Consistent Effort

Without consistency of effort you are doomed to fail. With consistency you can become a Superstar. Too many sales reps prospect and get some action going. As they are attending meetings and doing proposals, they stop the sales activity. Their income has the highs and the lows. This is a tough way to make a living.

How do you ensure consistency? Schedule the activities described previously so you make time every day. Pay attention to your numbers as previously described. Make sure you conduct your campaigns and calls to reach your goals. Your sales manager should hold you accountable. More importantly, you need to hold yourself accountable.

In summary, the Sales Potential Matrix is about growing business from current customers. Prospecting for Profit is about growing new business. We know sales reps who only focus on new business. Their service departments take care of current customers. Some reps only deal with current business, and still others sell to both current customers and new potential business.

Prospecting One More Time

Unfortunately many sales reps never prospect with power because they lack a system to track their efforts, as we have discussed here. They also lack discipline and persistence. Let's discuss each of these factors briefly.

You discipline yourself by organizing your schedule to make calls and other contact efforts regularly. Use a daily planner and put prospecting on your to-do list. One of our clients helps the reps out by using Dun and Bradstreet for their prospect lists. Then they have an assistant who loads all of their qualified prospect data into their CRM, which saves them time and effort. They set aside a SalesPower day once a week during which they make all of their calls. They use the rest of their week to visit potential customers face-to-face. Another client of ours requires 50 phone calls daily. A study of their metrics proves that with qualified prospects, they will secure eight to 10 quality appointments per week. What works for you in your job for you to be one of the best? The key is to schedule your time, all of the time, and to do the sales activity to get you there. Prospecting is the fuel that fires your sales engine. Without it, your sales career won't be able to get you anywhere.

Persistence separates the winners from the losers. More prospecting means more rejection, but remember: it isn't personal, it's just the way it is. Stay positive by reading the motivational messages in this book, listening to inspirational CDs, or studying other self-help books. Do whatever it takes to create the sort of mindset that will be free of frustration.

It will be tough at first, but network your way into an account. Whom do you know who knows somebody you want to know? Do an informational interview with that person or those people. Another good idea is to send a series of value-added, dynamic letters, followed by phone calls. Always make your calls professional and courteous. To help you contact new business, this book includes the following valuable resources:

▷ A sample phone call to a prospect.

▷ A sample letter to a prospect.

▷ An agenda for the first meeting with a new prospect.

Your level of professionalism will affect your rapport and credibility, so be well-prepared when approaching a customer on the phone, through letters, or by e-mail. These tools will work once the samples are modified to your industry and product.

> *To succeed in sales, simply talk to lots of people every day. And here's what's exciting—there are lots of people!*

—Jim Rohn

Sales Activity Reflection: Your Prospecting Power

Before we move onto ways of establishing rapport, it will be valuable for you to review your prospecting power. What sort of potential do you have that you should be using to your advantage? If you don't know the answer to that question, it's time to gauge just how much opportunity there is to pursue. Reflect on where you are when it comes to the five-step prospecting process.

1. Do you currently use a customer-relationship management system?

If so, identify two or three features you should learn or use more often.

If not, identify two customer-relationship management systems that fit your budget and meet your immediate needs that you can commit to considering.

---

2. On a scale of 1–10 (10 = all the time; 1 = never), how often do you use the resources you have available to you?

If you answered with a number between 1 and 5, identify three resources you need to use more often.

If you answered with a number between 6 and 10, identify one resource you need to use more often.

3. Do you know your numbers? Are you clear on your sales and income goals? Could you answer the questions on page 60? (If not, go back to the questions and answer them before continuing.)

4. Are you reviewing the numbers you ought to know, often enough?

If so, great job! Keep up the good work.

If not, how often would you like to review the numbers? Identify two to three concrete ways you can remind yourself to review them more often.

5. What percentage of your calendar is scheduled for meeting clients? For meeting prospects? In other words, how much time is organized into sections, time slots, or windows?

What's your goal for the amount of time scheduled?

What is one thing you can do immediately that will help you increase the percentage that's scheduled?

What is one thing you can do long term that will help you increase the percentage that's scheduled?

6. Identify one positive, self-help strategy you want to start, so that when frustration, disappointment, or rejection occurs, you have a strategy in mind to execute.

7. Take this last bit of space to really reflect on your abilities in the following areas: networking, discipline, organization, persistence, and metric retention. Write about where you are, where you want to be, and how you hope to get there. Believe in yourself and set SMART goals!

Buyer Roles, Decision Styles, and the Customer Buying Process

Buyer Roles

In most organizations, we see five key roles played out with regard to how decisions get made for the purchase and implementation of services and activities. Sometimes people play more than one role in a company. For example, in one of our accounts in the printing industry, the owner/president was also, unsurprisingly, the financial decision-maker. You only got to him if the user/influencer, the VP of sales, bought into your product and plan.

Following is a list of five common roles that we find played out within organizations that you will sell to. The list is intended to desribe the roles these individuals are fulfilling in the decision-making process. Your goal is to adapt and work with their role and process, rather than being caught by surprise.

1. The **financial decision-maker** is the person managing the account's budget. Usually someone in the purchasing department plays this role, but a purchasing team, an owner, or an individual with complete financial responsibility, such as a CFO, can also hold this position. Typically, this person makes the final spending decisions, such as approving a purchase, allocating money to a particular product, or agreeing to spend more than originally anticipated. This role is so critical that

if we don't know who the financial decision-maker is, we are operating blindly during the sales process. We need to understand the financial decision-maker's process, adapt our sales efforts accordingly, and be aware of the criteria he or she uses to make decisions.

2. The **user** is the individual who is implementing the product or service. Users are intimately involved with the product, especially from an application and technical perspective. They consider the solution's utility based on how it aligns with their needs; therefore, they are personally invested in the value of the offered solution.

3. The **influencer** is an expert who has substantial product knowledge and product experience. Influencers can be internal or external, or industry-recognized experts with a reputable status. Their influence is so inherently involved in the process that they are able to shape decisions without being present. Influencers' advice and opinions hold a lot of weight with customers.

4. The **doorkeeper** is the individual who allows (or disallows) access and insight into the process. Doorkeepers can be office managers, administrative assistants, or receptionists. A doorkeeper's *yes* may not influence the process, but a doorkeeper's *no* has the power to shut the door on a particular provider altogether. The person answering the phone has a lot of power because he or she has the authority to permit or withhold access.

5. The **guide/navigator** demystifies the organization and the roles that others play in the organizational setting. They can direct sales professionals to the real decision-makers and provide internal information that's critical to the purchasing decision. Having an effective guide or navigator is usually the difference between a successful sale and a lost sale that went awry during the process.

As a sales professional, your strategic goal is to ensure that you have an accurate understanding of the varying roles that influence the decision-making process, so that your sales activities align with and support these roles. Review the following chart to put this information to use. Superstar salespeople take action. So, apply this information to your next sales contact. Then do it again and again.

Buyer Roles

Financial Decision-Maker	User
• Has final approval on spending.	• Is affected by the need and the potential solution.
• Can veto.	
• Controls the money.	• Has a personal stake.
Influencer	**Doorkeeper**
• Is knowledgeable and/or experienced	• Decides who gets access.
• May be "staff" or outside "expert."	• Often has more influence than job/title suggests.
• May "shape" the decision without being present.	• Can say no and make it stick.

Guide/Navigator

Good ideas are common—what's uncommon are people who will work hard enough to bring them about.

—Ashleigh Brilliant

Sales Activity Reflection: Customer Roles in Decision-Making

Pick one customer and identify the individuals who influence that relationship. Make a few notes to yourself. If you get a chance, review this with a peer or your manager.

Notes:

Decision Styles

We recently had the experience of calling on a senior executive in a potential new global account. After receiving word that we had the business, we got a terrible surprise: The executive discovered that staff in the global headquarters wanted to talk to another company. He assured us that it was a formality. Later we discovered, along with him, that is was more than a formality. We ended up going through an extended and intensive effort to win the business, only to lose it in the end to a competitor that wasn't even on our radar. Obviously, there are times when you can't know what you can't know. But, shame on any of us who don't do everything we can to understand who is involved in the decision-making process and exactly how the decision will be made.

By understanding the decision-making process that will be used, we gain another strategic advantage in our selling process. Many sales are derailed because we have assumptions regarding how an organization will make decisions, so we inadvertently miss steps that would otherwise accommodate an organization's preferred decision-making style. Although there are a number of different decision styles, we will discuss the four primary styles that frequently play key roles in the decision-making process:

1. **Command:** One person is empowered to make the decision based on ownership, position, expertise, authority, or a combination of these factors.

2. **Consultative:** One person makes the decision after consulting others. Consulting may be done for support, advice, technical assistance, reputation purposes, and so forth. The information obtained during the consultation may or may not be utilized.

3. **Consensus, Collaboration, or Other Group Method:** We all make a decision that we mutually accept. Or, we vote to reach a majority.

4. **Laissez-Faire:** All users or practitioners make their decision and do their own thing.

Command

One person makes the decisions. Oftentimes, this person is an executive, such as a manager, managing partner, or COO. The authority to make the decision is based on the individual's expertise, level of ownership in the business, or status in the organization. In the command decision style, the goal is to find the person who makes the decision and convince that person that he or she should use your solution(s).

Consultative

Consultative decisions are made after consulting others. Consultation may be sought for any number of reasons, but it's important to remember that there's no guarantee that the input will be used. In a consultative decision–structured organization, it's helpful and important to determine who will be consulted and, if possible, the nature of the consultation. This way, we can seek to influence the person making the final decision and those who will be consulted.

Consensus, Collaboration, or Other Group Method

In many organizations, some sort of group-based decision-making style will be used formally or informally. Typically, it's this way for political reasons, considering the least amount of flack emerges when many people have been consulted, heard, or given the opportunity to influence. Although consensus decision-making can result in high-quality decisions, it can also delay the process. Decision-making becomes even more complex when an organization requires a unanimous decision, which requires everyone to agree upon a solution. By understanding a group's decision-making process, we can initiate relationships and attempt to influence both the individual and the group in the most favorable manner.

Laissez-Faire

This sort of decision-making occurs when individuals do their own thing. It's fairly common in professional settings where practitioners are assumed to have the expertise and rationale to decide on their own. In laissez-faire, it's more difficult to come to a consensus because all parties must use the same product offering.

The strategic-selling challenge includes understanding how organizations make decisions and accepting that there may not be only one decision-making process being used. Where is the customer in the decision-making process? Who will be making the decision? We want to match our selling activity to the customer's decision-making process.

Customer Buying Process

Interest: Something engages the customer; something catches the customer's attention. Maybe because the customer is actively searching for something in response to a need or perceived opportunity, or maybe because he or she just connects with a well-positioned piece of information.

Need or Opportunity: Individually or with the help of outside influence, the customer decides to pursue a perceived priority. This may be an active decision to pursue a need or opportunity, or it may be a passive open-mindedness that develops. The more positive expectation, curiosity, or pain, the more motivation the customer will have to "know."

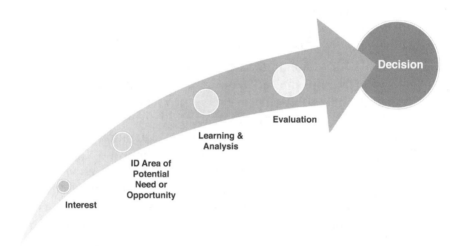

Learning and Analysis: Customers move into a stage of learning, educating themselves and analyzing. Driven by a combination of current knowledge (or lack thereof) and emotion, this stage centers on answering the following questions:

▷ How motivated am I to seek something to address this need or opportunity?

▷ How big is the gap between what I have and what I want?

▷ How much value is presented by alternative solutions?

▷ How much relief, satisfaction, or resolution will I receive in an alternative?

▷ Do I find the value compelling enough to act?

Evaluation: The evaluation stage is a dynamic interplay with the inquiry, adequacy of information, and perceived validity of the data sources discovered and examined in the learning and analysis stage. Evaluation moves along a continuum from "Is this worthy of any action at all?" to "How do I choose among the many undifferentiated choices available to me?" to "Is the value offered here equal to or greater than the alternatives?" or "I want this; how do I get it?" The interplay between the realization of a gap (need or opportunity), the attractiveness of the opportunities (presented or discovered), and the evaluation has the potential to result in a customer decision that holds a high degree of commitment. *Or, the customer may get lost in a sea of ambivalence.*

Decision: The final decision may be a decision *not* to decide, a "flip of a coin," or a committed decision (yes or no). A committed decision that fills the gap between the customer's need and the benefits of the solution provided is the ideal outcome of this process. And, commitment is generally a result of engagement in the learning and analysis stage and in evaluating the fit of the solution with a solid understanding of the impact of the need and/or the significance of the opportunity. When the dynamic interplay of these three difficult-to-navigate buyer stages has been fully and satisfactorily engaged by the customer, he or she will be in position to make a committed decision. Customers may be more inclined to have buyer's remorse or to simply back away from a decision when they aren't engaged enough to gain the insight needed to evaluate alternatives with an appropriate level of comfort. If they feel rushed through the process or the process is short-circuited by a salesperson who's mainly committed to making the sale, the customers will lack confidence in the decision and withdraw to minimize damage to their self-esteem and their business.

So What? Now What?

The key point in understanding this process is to understand that skillful customer engagement (by a sales professional)—recognizing where customers are in their process (the stage) and helping them effectively meet their needs (in each stage)—can help customers build confidence and commit to finding a solution that addresses their needs or opportunities. Doing this well may lead your customers to use your proposed solution. This is the essence of effective professional selling.

*The secret of person's success resides in his insight
into the moods of people, and his tact in dealing
with them.*

—J.G. Holland

Sales Activity Reflection: Decision Styles and Customer Buying Process

Identify three current accounts that you have worked with at some point. Where are you and where is the customer? Is there anything you can do to improve? For example, maybe you have been trying to close, but the customer is still asking for more pricing information or product options. In that case, you might need to identify what the customer needs, give it to him or her, and then close the sale.

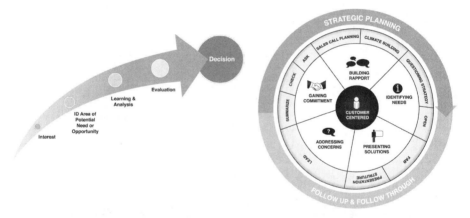

Customer Buying Process	Superstar Selling Process
Interest	Building Rapport
Identify Need or Opportunity	Identifying Needs
Learning and Analysis	Presenting Product Benefits
Evaluation	Addressing Customer Concerns
Decision	Closing the Sale

Customer, Decision Style, and Buying Stage	Sales Professional Approach and Sales Phase	Improvement
1.		
2.		
3.		

Sales Relationship Map

In this section, we will discuss five different conceptual positions that you may occupy within a customer relationship. Each position is descriptive. It references a set of guideposts that help us to see where we are in the relationship, and it is also instructive because it helps us identify key strategies that can help us strengthen our relationship and improve our ability to sell. Overall, then, the map offers guidance on how to design our sales approach in order to achieve a more favorable relationship with the customer.

We will consider each of the five positions and discuss the ease and amount of access that's implied, the areas of tension and influence, and the available knowledge we have about our customer and our company. Finally, we will use that information to identify the appropriate sales strategy needed to advance.

The ideal pathway into any relationship is one in which you meet, get acquainted, find common interests and values, and, over time, deepen the relationship so that each finds a place of safety and value. The same is true in a business relationship. Ideally, there is an initiation to the relationship that brings the sales professional into initial connection with the customer.

This "getting acquainted and mutual exploration" process moves to some exploration of possibilities, resulting in some deepening of the relationship to include some initial conduct of business and validation of the fit between the sales professional and customer. Deepening learning and trust results in a willingness to invest in a deeper business relationship and stronger interdependence, until finally the sales professional earns status

Sales Relationship Map

Sales Relationship Map

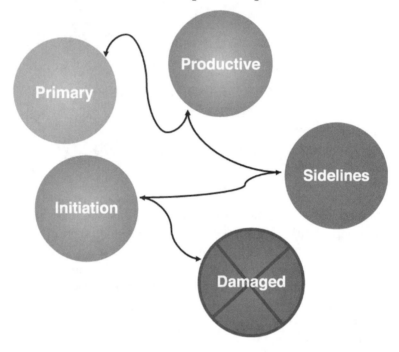

as a highly dependable and central contributor to the customer's business. This progression is easy to imagine and describe, but in actual practice, each step is unique and highly unpredictable.

Changing business conditions, varied skills and agendas within each organization, and competing goals and objectives influence relationships and affect the time and trajectory of the movement on the map. Whereas the ideal destination for the sales professional is to achieve productive or primary status with each of their customers, the reality is that each of their competitors is seeking a similar status in the same organizations. Your organization's capabilities and past history, as well as the changing personalities and relationships with you and your colleagues, all have a dynamic impact on these outcomes. And, although we don't like to face it and spend a lot of time on it, in reality, many things may damage your relationship with your customer and impact your ability to move your organization into a stronger position of trust and capability required to be a primary player in his or her business.

Here is a working description of what it means to you as a salesperson to occupy each of the positions on the sales relationship map, and how you can "read the map" to identify steps you can take to improve your status in order to win a stronger position and win more business. We will start with a description of a damaged relationship because, even though it's not a desirable position to occupy in any customer relationship, we all need to know how to avoid it and what to do to improve our situation if we find ourselves there.

Damaged

A damaged relationship can occur in various situations, but it's usually the by-product of falling out of favor with an account. Frequent billing mistakes, product failures, delivery problems, and administration issues may be responsible for creating tension between you and the key decision-makers.

When you're in a damaged selling relationship, your access to the account is very limited, if not completely restricted. This lack of access makes it extremely difficult to change the quality of the relationship, secure an approachable position, generate a flow of information, and influence effectively. At the same time, the negative feelings and lack of communication make it challenging to change the account's perspective of our company. Trust is minimal, so any information that's exchanged is generally held with a critical frame of reference.

To repair a damaged relationship, the sales strategy must focus on eliminating negative feelings and working from a clean slate. Two of the best strategies include apologizing appropriately for real or imagined shortcomings, and committing to "making it right." This usually includes confronting the need to change and committing to improve quality in the future. After you have reestablished rapport, you may need to replace personalities who have not mixed well with the client (including yourself). Making a change must be the primary focus of your strategy. Often it's necessary to uncover old wounds if you hope to discuss expectations, repair the damage, and renegotiate the relationship.

Repairing damaged relationships often requires a lot of time and energy to determine if it's worth it to pursue its repair. One rationale that encourages this approach is the reality that dissatisfied customers generally share their unhappiness with others. Because of this, there's a very real risk that our damaged relationship with one account might damage other existing account relationships.

Initiation

Initiation is meant to describe a new relationship, as well as situations in which we are trying to build relationships with brand-new accounts or accounts that we have not pursued yet. Networking your way into a new relationship is one of the better ways to access brand-new accounts. Sometimes access is available through professional courtesy if our company has a positive reputation in the marketplace. Your influence in these relationships is minimal, although influence may generate from the image our company holds in the industry. During this stage, your knowledge of the customer is limited and often somewhat superficial.

Initiation

- Pursuing a new relationship.
- You have no current business with this customer.
- You have no significant relationships in the business.
- Your ability to influence is negotiable.
- Your knowledge of the business is insignificant.
- The customer's knowledge of your offerings is suspect.

What strategy must you utilize to sell and progress in this position?

This sales strategy is one that requires fairly persistent relationship-building activity, followed by a thorough needs identification process and an intentional establishment of trust. This strategy may involve a series of small steps before a strong relationship is possible.

Sidelines

This position is similar to being on the sidelines in a sporting situation. Consider this: You have made the cut and you're on the team, but at this point you've been relegated to a secondary position, so you are on the bench most of the time. At this point, your competitor has a better track record than you and, until you prove you're deserving, the coach is going to give you limited playing time.

Your access has increased since the initiation phase, but it's still significantly less than that of your competitors. The competition may still be the vendor of choice because they have established comfortable relationships within the organization. Yet, if you persist, you can develop a stronger position of influence and advocacy. Even though your knowledge of the customer and your customer's knowledge of you are growing, you're still relatively insignificant to the customer.

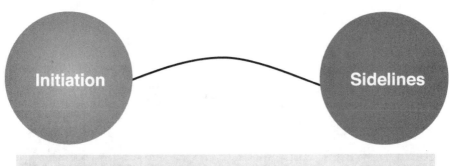

- You've advanced in the relationship.
- You have some productive relationships.
- You may have some level of advocacy in the organization.
- You have been able to learn about the business and the main stakeholders.

What strategy must you utilize to sell and progress in this position?

At this point, the sales strategy is to consistently call on the account, continue to expand the access, and, thereby, expand your influence. The biggest challenge is to win the opportunity to be seen and then take full advantage of it. When you get in the game by winning demonstrations, building credibility with your company experts, and selling related products, the pressure to deliver increases considerably. This helps you to further increase your visibility and viability within the account.

Productive

You've established a productive relationship when you're regularly talking to and meeting with the client. The relationship should be growing, your access to the account should be easier, and your influence and advocacy within the organization should be expanding. At this stage, you need to use your team to solidify your credibility and trust with the account.

The increased access and strengthened relationships create a more natural flow of information between you and the key employees in the organization. This adds to your ability to influence and to advocate within the customer's organization. The significance of this position stems from taking full advantage of the access to deepen your business knowledge, both at the product and the service levels. Doing this allows you to use that information as a leverage to deliver an on-target proposal at the right time.

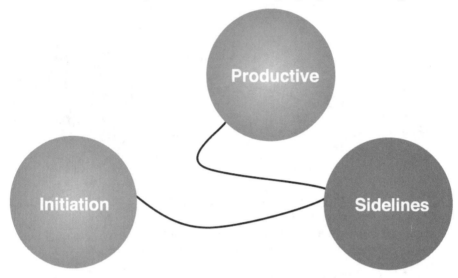

- You've established a relationship that's generating business.
- You are winning profitable business.
- You know the right stakeholders in the business.
- The account knows you.
- You have a position that's increasingly influential.

What strategy must you utilize to sell and progress in this position?

Price may be more sensitive here than at previous stages. By this point, competitors may be awakened to your presence and determined to prevent your attempts at building the relationship. High-quality, professional presentations, legendary follow-through, and prompt responses to requests are all critical at this stage.

Primary

This final position is one in which you and your company maintain a prominent presence with an account. You have gained virtually all of the profitable business that you want, and information flows freely and frequently. Access is complete, so you are considered a member of the team, and it's understood that you are a key player in the organization. Your influence is high, your ability to advocate is high, and the mutual knowledge between you and your account is high.

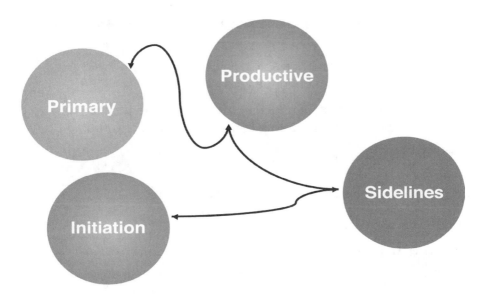

This sales strategy needed at this position in the relationship is focused on protecting your existing position and continuing to explore new opportunities with further potential. High-quality, problem-free results are crucial. Also, transitioning from sales to service in any company is essential. You must continue to follow through on your promises, communicate clearly to your company support team, and anticipate organizational needs and problems. This is the ticket to maintaining full partnership; otherwise, your hard work to land the account will be wasted, and you'll risk becoming vulnerable like a past vendor.

Obviously, the goal is to be a primary player in all of your key accounts. If you hope to maximize your potential, you must know your position in each account, set your sales strategies accordingly, and continue to feed the pipeline. You should always have a diverse mix of customers, some at the initiation, sideline, and productive stages, in order to achieve your sales goals. You must continue to secure your position in each account, and remember that neglect can lead to competitor intrusion. One final and important truism is that it's only a short distance from any of the positive relationships on the map to a damaged relationship, unless you are continuing to manage and attend to your accounts.

Sales Relationship Map

> The goal is to be a primary or secondary player in all of your accounts.

> Know your position in the account and set your sales strategy accordingly.

> Continue to feed the pipeline to maximize your territory potential. This requires an ongoing effort to initiate new accounts.

> Strive to secure your position in the account. Any neglect gives your competitors an opportunity to intrude.

> Without continuous management, it doesn't take much to turn a productive relationship into a damaged relationship.

Sales Relationship Map Definitions

Initiation

▷ Do your homework. Review annual reports, use the Internet, and read articles about the individual or company you plan to meet.

▷ Learn about the company and its decision-making process, culture, and history.

▷ Build relationships. Get to know others and help them get to know you.

▷ Learn about their industry, business goals, and vision.

▷ Focus on identifying their needs and priorities.

▷ Present high-quality literature and/or a professional presentation.

Sidelines

▷ Continue to build on your knowledge of the company.

▷ Continue to network your way into the organization.

▷ Be mindful that everything you do impacts your image and your company's brand.

▷ Ask, listen, and learn. Watch for obvious and subtle cues that will guide you forward.

▷ Though you need to establish your credibility, don't be tempted to present too soon.

▷ Remember, they may give you a small piece of business to test your capability.

▷ Be consistent with your follow-through.

▷ Send articles, e-mails, and updates to continue to build influence.

▷ If you get an opportunity to win some business, make sure that you make a good first impression by starting strong.

Productive

▷ Given that you're probably competing against other major players, your price and quality of work are pivotal to your ability to win the account.

▷ Remain close to your major contacts and listen to their guidance and feedback.

▷ Communicate clearly to your support team, updating them on expectations, needs, and promises that you've made to the account.

▷ Maintain and continue building the close personal relationships responsible for getting you where you are.

▷ Look for opportunities to deliver the solution and to meet with key stakeholders.

▷ Ensure that you're well prepared to hold results-focused meetings every time you engage with them.

Primary

▷ Quality and delivery will determine your success moving forward.

▷ Maintain contact throughout the delivery of the contract so that you maintain your position for future opportunity with the client.

▷ Remember, you are now the target of all of your competitors.

Damaged

▷ You have made a mistake.

▷ Relationships are damaged, and the business is in jeopardy.

▷ You must mend the relationships in question.

▷ Determine what caused the problem and seek to get the issue corrected.

▷ Take responsibility for your mistakes, apologize, and identify an equitable resolution.

▷ Work to reestablish relationships and look for ways to rebuild credibility.

▷ Ensure that you explain what you've changed, so that the problem doesn't reoccur.

▷ Invest the necessary time and money required.

Sales Activity Reflection: Sales Relationship Map

Select a current account and complete the following chart. (Note: Use these Sales Activity Reflections as practice, drill, and rehearse.) All sales champions are better prepared in the sales goals/plans and competence than their competitors.

Account name:
Position on the map:
Indicators that you're in that position:
Strategies to improve your position:
Risks to consider on this account, in this position:

We succeed in enterprises which demand the positive qualities we possess, but we excel in those which can also make use of our defects.

—Alexis de Tocqueville

DAY 9

Strategic Sales Planning: SWOT Analysis

You have identified the right customer target and have gained extensive knowledge of the prospect or current customers. You have developed relationships with the right players and have determined the roles they play in the decision-making process. You have deciphered the motivational preferences of each decision-maker, and you've analyzed the organization's preferred decision style. Now you are well-positioned to do a practical analysis of the organization.

Strategic sales planning is a process of reviewing the pluses and minuses of your market or territory. It's a big picture, or macro, view of your selling potential and challenges. Individual sales-call planning (which we will review later) focuses on one account, one sales call, and the plan you have for it. This is a micro view of sales planning. Or it can focus on your strategy for one key account.

Using a SWOT analysis you methodically review strengths, weaknesses, opportunities, and threats are commonly assessed to analyze a business. Usually you do this once a year.

Initiating strengths-focused conversations with a variety of decision-makers or sales reps in your company gives you an opportunity to see what strengths drive a business's success. Similar conversations focused on weaknesses, opportunities and threats will give you important data to consider when forming your sales strategy. You can do this alone, but input from others gives you added perspective and prevents narrow thinking and tunnel vision.

Why Use SWOT?

SWOT

A SWOT analysis is a helpful framework that identifies strengths and weaknesses while examining existing opportunities and threats. Completing a SWOT analysis helps you focus your activities on areas where you are strong and where the greatest opportunities exist.

Strengths

▷ What advantages do your customers have?

▷ What do your customers do well?

▷ What resources are available to your customers?

Keep in mind that you may see strengths that your customers do not. Consider their strengths in relation to their competitors' strengths.

Weaknesses

▷ What could your customers improve?

▷ What do you think they do poorly?

Again, consider this from their stance as well as from your professional perspective. Do their own customers seem to recognize weaknesses that they don't? Are their competitors doing better than them?

Opportunities

▷ What good opportunities are present?

▷ What trends are you are aware of?

Useful opportunities can emerge when changes take place in technology, market trends, social systems, lifestyle preferences, and population patterns. Also, local events should be considered when evaluating potential opportunities. A useful approach is to review the strengths, and then determine whether these strengths create opportunities. Alternatively, consider your customers' weaknesses to decide whether opportunities exist if you can eliminate the weaknesses.

Threats

▷ What obstacles do your customers face?

▷ What is their competition doing?

▷ Are technology changes threatening their position?

Oftentimes, completing this analysis will help to identify what needs to be done and to put problems into perspective.

> *Strategic plans are often worthless, but planning is absolutely essential.*
>
> —Peter Drucker

Sales Activity Refection: SWOT in Sales Planning

Complete this in-depth SWOT planning tool for your sales activities. It will help you focus on your priority sales opportunities in the markets you serve. We have learned that Superstars plan more effectively than other reps.

Customer Needs

Key Considerations:
- Past or Current Sales Problems/Complaints
- Decision-Making Process
- Relationship to Decision-Makers
- The Customer's Marketing Efforts
- Knowledge of Industry Products and/or Software
- Use of Marketing Support Efforts
- Business Issues/Goals/Success Measures
- Other:

Strengths?	Weaknesses?
Opportunities?	Threats?

Competitive Review

Key Considerations:
- Top Competitors
- Competitors' Strengths and Weaknesses
- Market Strategies and Impact
- Position With Top Accounts
- Other:

Strengths?	Weaknesses?
Opportunities?	Threats?

Current Business Situation

Key Considerations:
- YTD Sales vs. Goals
- Volume of Business vs. Potential Volume
- Relationships With Customers
- The Reason Customers Buy From You
- Price vs. Value
- Product Benefits
- Other:

Strengths?	Weaknesses?
Opportunities?	Threats?

Marketing Support

Key Considerations:
- Company Literature
- Company Website
- Customer Incentive Programs
- Demonstrations/Presentations
- Marketing Materials
- Training
- Other:

Strengths?	Weaknesses?
Opportunities?	Threats?

Sales Teamwork

Key Considerations:
- Internal and External Sales Communication
- Job Roles and Expectations
- Problem-Solving Complaints
- Commitment Follow-Through
- Procedure Effectiveness
- Training and Meetings
- Other:

Strengths?	Weaknesses?
Opportunities?	Threats?

Strategic Goals and Plans
• Priority Strengths (top 3–5)
• Priority Weaknesses to Improve (top 2–3)
• Priority Opportunities (top 3–5)
• Top Threats to Neutralize (top 2–3)

SMART Goals and Action Steps
1.Business Volume and Profitability
Action Steps?
2.Targeted Contacts and Marketing Strategies
Action Steps?
3.Other Goals
Action Steps?

Summary

Through this process, you ought to be focusing on one customer and planning how to approach him or her based on your planning efforts. As opposed to shooting from the hip, top sales professionals have a game plan for each customer visit. This means planning your approach for each step of the sales process. (We will review this more later, too.) Both the overall sales planning and sales call planning are vital steps to put yourself in a position where you can establish credible rapport with prospects.

Here's a review of the sales process steps:

▷ Call objectives.

▷ Building rapport.

▷ Identifying needs.

▷ Presenting product benefits.

▷ Addressing concerns.

▷ Closing the sale.

▷ Follow-up and follow-through.

Finally, make sure to document what happened, taking note of the next steps that should be done in order to meet the customer's needs. With a little extra foresight and effort, sales professionals can master this part of the Superstar selling model to gain an edge over the competitors that are vying for the customer's business. Today, most big companies have all of this automated through sales contact management software. If your company doesn't, you can take the lead now that you have this information.

> *What helps luck is a habit of watching for*
> *opportunities, of having a patient but restless mind,*
> *of sacrificing one's ease or vanity, or uniting a love*
> *of detail to foresight, and of passing through hard*
> *times bravely and cheerfully.*
>
> —Victor Cherbuliez

How to Be a Winner

Success is indeed a state of mind. Winning is a state of mind. Successful selling is a habit that can be cultivated through intentional training and positive perspective. It's similar to a farmer's attitude about his crops. Obstacles will emerge, and the farmer will face hazardous weather, pests, and market deviations; however, the successful farmer is persistent, day-by-day and season-by-season. Similarly, Superstars remain dedicated, regardless of the product, customer, or market condition.

So, How Do Winners Succeed?

Winners go within. They imagine the best, not the worst. They think about what they want, not what they don't want; they pre-play positives rather than ruminate over the negatives. Winners create the futures they want and don't dwell on past mistakes or lost opportunities. They practice relentlessly and act persistently to achieve perfection. Attitudes, images, and commitments are pivotal to achieving peak performance.

Dick Fosbury, inventor of the Fosbury Flop, used his imagination and discipline to set a high-jump world record of 7 feet 3 inches and to win a 1968 Olympic gold medal. He'd rock back and forth a few times to spur his run and jump, and then he'd run and high jump backward over the bar.[1] He was a world champion—a winner! All champions train intensely and imagine positively. Jean-Claude Killy won three Olympic gold medals using this technology. Jack Nicklaus, Tom Watson, Gary Player, and Tiger Woods visualize a golf shot before they swing.[2] Why? It refocuses them on their best form instead of leaving their attention on previous errors.

Astronauts are some of the most exceptional examples of this discipline. Nobody really knew what the Apollo moon expeditions would be like, except maybe Jules Verne or Ray Bradbury; however, the astronauts performed their tasks with precision. They spent thousands of hours practicing in the desert and the ocean. They replayed the desired end result with NASA simulations. In fact, Neil Armstrong even said the moon expedition was "beautiful, just like the drill."[3]

Do you face obstacles? Sure! But, so did the POWs in Vietnam. Many spent years behind bars, deprived of physical comforts and intellectual activity. To fight boredom, they took self-development into their own hands by mentally challenging themselves.[4]

Do you want to be a winner and achieve sales excellence? Start imagining superior results and successful sales. Continue to learn during every training session and customer interaction. Finally, remember to be persistent, to act as a team player, and to know your numbers. Watch your sales and income increase!

> *Forget about the business outlook, be on the outlook for business.*
>
> —Paul J. Meyer

Sales Activity Reflection: See Yourself Winning

If success is really a state of mind, how do you feel about your current frame of mind? Are you doing the internal, intellectual imaginative exercises that will help make your success a reality? We hope so! Do you see yourself as a success? We hope so!

In order to help you get to a place where seeing yourself as a success becomes second nature, we invite you to take 10–15 minutes to complete the following meditation practice.

1. Find a quiet place that's free of other people and distractions.

2. Pick one thing in your life (make it very specific) that you want to accomplish.

3. Close your eyes. Imagine yourself getting into your car. Put whatever "it" is in the direction of north. Anything east, west, or south is away from "it."

4. You start your car, you know your destination, and you begin your journey. As you head north, an intense wind heads in your direction. It's not in your favor; in fact, it's keeping your car from continuing north. You stop your car, you take a walk, you think about what "it" is that's waiting for you, and you get back into your car. *Take a moment here to imagine doing each one of these things. Stop. Walk. Think. Restart.*

5. You pull into a rental car agency that's right off the road. You swap your little two-door for a large, heavyweight pick-up truck. You know the high winds won't be able to stop this vehicle.

6. You get back on the road and embrace the winds. Two hundred miles later, there's a detour. You can't continue directly north. You have to head one of two ways: east or northeast. The northeast detour takes much longer, but it's still heading halfway in the direction you want to go. So, you take it. It's a dirt road that's full of potholes you must dodge, slower speeds you must accommodate, and less scenery you can enjoy.

7. The journey is long. You get tired. You get hungry. And for most of the ride, there's no service on your phone or reception on your radio. You have no one to talk to or keep you busy. You start to wonder if it's worth it. So you stop, take a walk to rouse yourself, and get some fuel for your car and your stomach.

8. You feel refreshed; you get back on the road. After five long days, the detour finally starts to head north again. You get excited as you remember what "it" is you've traveled all this way to accomplish.

9. You are heading due north, and you see a sign that reads "'IT'—THIRTY MILES." You can't believe it; you're almost there! Five miles later your pick-up truck dies. Something in the engine went wrong. You cannot believe that you've made it all this way, only to be left without a way to travel to "it." You sit on the side of the road and you begin to sob. You get angry. You feel defeated. You feel lost and afraid and every other emotion, all at once.

10. You tell yourself to take a few breaths, and you do. You gather your thoughts. You compose yourself. And you decide: You haven't come this far to let "it" go.

11. You begin to walk. You know that if you keep reminding yourself of how important "it" is to you, you will find the energy to walk every single step of the next 25 miles. You walk for hours and hours. The daylight leaves, and you're left in darkness. Finally, you see a sign that reads "'IT'—2 MILES."

12. You start to run. No matter how tired you feel or how exhausted your body is, you dig deep to use every last ounce of energy to make your legs move as fast as they are able. And you run. You are sprinting. And then, you see "it." "It" is now within mere feet of you. You stop.

13. You want to take "it" in. You take a minute to remind yourself of the journey. The wind, the detour, the car exchange, the exhaustion, and the hunger. You decide that every minor disappointment was worth it; you have reached your destination. "It" is yours.

14. You take your final steps to reach "it." And you think, "I've made it!"

15. Take five minutes to write your thoughts about this imaginative exercise. How did you feel when you envisioned yourself experiencing this journey? How did you feel when you reached your goal and achieved "it"?

Building Rapport

Y ou must understand and constantly review the dynamics of the sales process in order to successfully offer customers the products and services that meet their needs. Although all steps are important, if you're not able to build trust and rapport, you will be finished at this step. Without rapport, your customers will doubt, resent, and reject you. With it, you earn the opportunity to continue the sales process by gaining their trust, confidence, and business.

Relate, Focus, and Check

You have done your homework, and now you are on the phone or face-to-face with the customer. Now what? How do you use your knowledge and plan effectively?

Whenever two people get together, a climate is created. It is not physical but attitudinal in nature. You do certain things that make it positive or negative. Many times you are not even aware of how you affect the customer. The more positive actions you take, the more rapport and trust you will build with the customer. Three key actions help you do this quickly and professionally: relate, focus, and check.

Relate

Relating is a process that involves getting acquainted, building a working relationship, making friends, and establishing credibility with a customer. Take these steps to begin relating and building rapport:

• Be prepared. • Be on time. • Smile and shake hands firmly. • Make eye contact. • Introduce yourself.	• Be courteous and use good manners. • Ask for his or her name. • Look sharp/dress appropriately. • Engage in pleasant small talk. • Listen closely.

Focus and Check:

After you have established a professional presence and connection, you need to focus on your original purpose for the customer contact. You may have already established this during prior discussions, but you need to reconfirm to verify that your agenda is the same as the customer's agenda. Gain agreement early. For example:

> "Mrs. Jones, you've indicated to your business development manager that you're interested in exploring a partnership with our company. With your permission, I'd like to get to know you more by asking you a number of questions that will help me learn about you and your needs. After understanding this, we can focus on the extensive product options that we could offer you through our distribution. Then, I'd like to review some market data I have for you. This way, I can identify the most effective way that I can be of service to you. Do you mind if I proceed according to that plan?"

Most of the time, if you have done your homework, the customer will agree with your plan. Your goal is to make sure you and the customer are on the same page. If you are planning to go one direction and the customer is going the other, it will be a tough appointment. Also, this simple communication technique gives your customer the chance to add an extra objective that you may need to know to successfully offer and deliver the service that's needed. Occasionally there might be an unexpected problem to solve before you get to your agenda.

Building rapport is similar to laying the foundation of a building. Although there is still work to do after it's laid, a solid foundation provides critical support to the rest of the structure. Your main objectives during this step are to reduce tension and to create a positive climate with your customer. Your thinking should be focused on what you can do to make customers feel comfortable when discussing their most pressing needs. This is often done through the simple, yet significant, steps we have already described. However, the steps must be crafted delicately and uniquely to fit each unique customer contact.

The biggest barrier to completing a sale is often distrust. Take time to get to know more about your customer, be sincere, thoroughly prepare, and approach the customer professionally, and you will have a good start. Customers will buy from you because they like you and they feel understood by you—not because they entirely understand your products or services. Building rapport is a process of creating trust. You should constantly be working on this during the sales process. Think of how you treat your closest friends, and then show your customers the same level of respect. They will be more likely to share their situation with you, remain interested in working with you, and develop a long-term, profitable partnership with you. Every step in the sales process either adds to or detracts from your customer rapport.

Here are the top 10 sales mistakes that lose trust and cost you in lost sales and income:

1. **Lack of preparation.** There is nothing worse than a sales rep who doesn't know anything about a customer, hasn't prepared for a presentation, and lacks brochures or demo material. It projects amateurism and a poor overall approach.

2. **Doesn't listen.** Most reps today are product peddlers who have already decided what to sell even before they talk to an account. More sales are lost due to poor listening habits and questioning skills than any other sale mistake.

3. **Manipulation.** Some reps try to win business through coercion, deception, name-dropping, and favors. First of all, there are no ethics represented here, and it is the wrong way to do business. Second, trying to buy business with trips, golf outings, fancy dinners, or other such perks is dinosaur thinking. Many companies have policies against this kind of behavior. Various unscrupulous salespeople in Ponzi schemes, junk bonds, real estate, and other industries are in prison because of their efforts.

4. **Premature presentation.** One salesperson we came across had record-breaking proposals for a company. However, he ended up not making many sales. The problem was that he wrote a proposal for every meeting he had. What he didn't do was a good job at identifying the customer's need. We have learned it's best to wait, and make your presentation only after you have asked all key questions that you might need to ask in order to fully understand the customer's needs. You also should be sure to confirm each need with the customer and ensure that the customer has a real desire to do something about it. Only then are you really positioned to make a successful proposal.

5. **Needless approach.** Poor questioning and listening skills can lead to a misidentification of what the customer needs or wants. Then, an inappropriate presentation is made. Need confirmation can prevent this from occurring in most cases.

6. **No budget.** Many sales are lost because reps forget to ask for or clarify a budget range. This results in their proposal being way out of line: either too cheap or too expensive for a customer.

7. **No decision-maker involved.** If you don't talk to the decision-maker, your chances of success dwindle.

8. **Poor closing skills.** The Superstar selling process is a system that builds customer confirmation every step of the way. Closing a customer is about confirming an agreement, not forcing a customer to make a decision.

9. **Professional visitor.** Many reps are nice people and the customers like them. However, they never get down to business. The goal in sales is to fulfill a legitimate need that will create a loyal customer by offering a solution in exchange for money.

10. **Lack of follow-up.** This one is a no-brainer, but it causes many lost sales because a salesperson doesn't follow through. This mistake can involve not keeping commitments or promises. It can also involve a lack of keeping in touch with current customers or prospects.

It is not your customer's job to remember you. It is your obligation and responsibility to make sure they don't have the chance to forget you.

—Patricia Fripp

Sales Activity Reflection: Sales Call Preparation

Use this as a guide to plan an individual sales call. Or use any of the accounts you've used in other sales activities. Remember, winning isn't everything; the will to prepare to win is everything. You plan so that you're prepared to think on your feet.

So, take 15–20 minutes to plan an actual sales call with a current customer prospect to get an idea of what things to ask, consider, and do when conducting a real, live call. Practicing this plan *will* prepare you so it is "live action." Superstar salespeople have a plan, and they execute better than others. All you need to do is outline some notes to yourself. This is taking the macro plan you created earlier and putting it into practice on one sales call. Do this kind of sales-call planning every time, and over time it will become an unconscious great habit. We have used this in our management consulting practice to win millions of dollars in business.

Account Details: Name/Number
Build Rapport—Relate, Focus, and Check
Identify Needs—Exploratory Questions
Present Solution: FAB

Address Concerns-LEAD
Potential Concerns (Potential Responses)
Close the Sale—Recap Needs, Review Key Benefits, Ask for the Sale
Post-Call Review—Objective Achieved?
Opportunities Identified:

Sample Telephone Call to a Prospect

i. Introduction and Opening

"Mr. Jones?" *(pause for yes response)* "Good morning! This is *Sarah* with *ABC Company.* I'm glad I reached you! Do you have a quick minute to talk? My *(special)* reason for calling today is...."

- Add a pleasantry before "reason for calling today is."
- Be positive and upbeat.
- Use his name and give your name.
- Tell him you've done some homework.
- Tell him that you've thought about him and his particular business situation.

ii. Gain Interest With a Benefit or a Hook

For example: Personalize the statement to your industry.

- "We are creating exciting, new programs that go far beyond what you may have with your current product or service."
- "In today's competitive marketplace, the results your employees produce can have a major impact on attracting new business. *(pause)* Our company provides incentives that attract new contacts to your office to help your business grow."
- "We have some new and unique product styles that we are really excited about, and I thought you might be interested."

iii. Schedule and Ask for an Appointment

- "Would *(day/time)* be convenient to meet for 30 minutes to discuss our approach?"
- "Would Tuesday or Thursday a.m. be more convenient to meet for 30 minutes?"
- "Mr. Jones, could we meet for approximately 30 minutes next Wednesday?"
- "We could evaluate this in about 30 minutes. Would Monday or Wednesday afternoon work for you?"

Sample Letter or E-Mail to a Prospect

Your Name
Your Address
City, State, and Zip

Today's Date

Ms. President of XYZ Company
Street Address
City, State, and Zip

Dear Ms. President:

ABC Company has won the Consumer Choice Award eight years in a row as the best company in our industry! *(The goal with this sentence is to grab the recipient's attention. This heading can be up to 10–12 words.)*

At *ABC*, we have worked with a number of companies in the *retail* industry, and we have successfully helped them to: *(Relate to market/prospect needs.)*

- Improve their company image.
- Enhance their safety.
- Increase their employee morale.

Currently, we are working with many other reputable companies, which include: *DEF Company, MNO Company,* and *RST Company,* to name a few. *(Pick other companies that would be relevant to their industry.)*

Within the next three days, I will call you to arrange an appointment. During this meeting, we can clarify your priorities, review what I've learned about your organization, and highlight your potential options. *(Focus on successfully meeting their business needs and ask for an appointment.)*

Sincerely,

Your Name
ABC Company

P.S. I have attached a testimonial letter from one of our key customers at *IJK Company. (Always provide them with a little something extra.)*

Sample Outline for Initial Meeting With a Prospect (30 Minutes)

a. Introduction
- Relate.
- Focus.
- Check.

b. Use the OPEN Model to Clarify Needs
- Check to ensure you have correctly understood the customer's expressed needs.

c. Make a Power-Selling Statement
- Tailor this to the customer's needs and the benefits of using your company.
- *Mrs. President, we have worked with DEF Company for 15 years, and through our program, we have helped them to improve their image. They will be the first to tell you that we're highly responsive to ever-changing needs and market trends.*

d. Give a High-Level Overview of Capabilities

e. Ask for Questions

f. Suggest a New Step

g. Thank the Customer and Close the Meeting

h. Follow Up
- Send a thank-you note to let them know you appreciated his or her time.
- Send an e-mail or letter to summarize the conversation that took place.

Strive for excellence, not perfection.

—H. Jackson Brown, Jr.

Sales Activity Reflection: Make a Sample Reality

Now that you have seen various examples of sample calls, e-mails, and letters, it's your turn! Take 30–45 minutes to create your own call outline, e-mail, or letter for an actual client. Take your time and do it right. This is something you will want to really use with a client, so don't waste the time on something you won't apply. When you are done creating your real-life sample, answer these questions so that you can reference them in the future when you complete this process again (and again and again):

1. Why did you choose the format you chose?

2. What are two or three things that you think would be important to take into consideration when putting together a call outline, e-mail, or letter in the future?

3. What's one thing you learned during this process that you hadn't previously considered?

4. How will you apply that learning in the future?

5. What was difficult when you were creating this real-life sample?

6. What did you enjoy about creating a real-life sample?

Identifying Needs

Focus on the customer instead of yourself! Just as we are, customers are motivated by what they need. So, identifying needs successfully allows us to give the customers what they want, which ultimately means that we get what we want, too. Focus on your customer, not your sale.

Nearly every customer's purchase is an attempt to solve a problem or satisfy a need. This step is one of the most important because, if it's done properly, it positions you to address real, viable, high-priority customer needs. If it's done poorly, your presentation will likely be scattered, disorganized, and arbitrary. This step can transform an average sales professional into a consultant who's able to offer high-impact solutions instead of razzle-dazzle remedies that say all the right things but fail to deliver anything. This step is about identifying and addressing the customer's priorities.

To understand the physical and personal concerns of the customer, you can strategically ask the customer questions. An outcome is successful when a product or service is identified as the solution to a customer's concerns or objectives. This step should answer this question: *How can I listen more effectively to understand the customer's real needs?*

Pull, Push, and Move Away Strategies

As salespeople reflect on the influence they have on customers, they ought to ask: *Do I know what it would be like for me to be on the other side of my sales efforts?* In other words, can you determine how you affect others?

To have a positive influence means that your approach is constructive and respectful. This means that you don't have any hidden agendas, but that you have integrity; you believe in your goals and what they represent. There are three different strategies to explain the different ways of navigating communication:

Push: Whenever you are advancing your own agenda, you are using a push strategy. You are willing to tell others directly what you want, persuade them, convince them with evidence, or entice them with logic. Essentially, if you are focused on accomplishing your own agenda, you are in push mode.

Pull: Whenever you are authentically establishing common ground, actively listening, or supporting areas of agreement, you are using pull energy. You are willing to be influenced by others when you're in this mode.

Move Away: We can move away for two reasons. If we temporarily disengage, we are typically trying to think, refocus, or buy time, with the intention of returning our attention at some point. Examples include walking away from a car dealer during negotiations, and taking a break when tension escalates during a meeting. The second type of moving away occurs when we are diplomatically trying to avoid something that has become a distraction to our priorities.

In the United States, we tend to value the push strategy. We are an achievement-oriented culture, and push is the straightforward way to get from point A to point B. In business situations, we tend to want to fight every battle and tackle every issue. We are not terribly judicious when it comes to moving away from some things to focus on other, more important issues. Typically, when we need to influence, we are more likely to be *in someone's face* than we are to move away.

Identifying needs is primarily a pull strategy. It works best when orchestrated with skill and authentic concern regarding the customer's needs. Without concern, the very same skill set and methodology can become manipulative and ineffective; at best, it can feel like a scam to the customer. The strategy of questions identifies and understands customers' problems, hopes, and concerns.

The most effective way to approach the identifying needs process is to initiate general conversation that focuses on isolating the priorities that need attention. Much like a funnel, the questions begin with information that you have gathered during the pre-visit planning and then progress toward understanding more specific needs.

As you can see, there are advantages to each strategy, depending on the scenario, the client, and the goal. So the real question is: *What's it like to be on the other side of your sales efforts?* As you read these questions consider the customer's point of view.

1. After reading the previous section, which strategy resonated with you the most?

2. Why were you drawn to that particular strategy? List at least two reasons.

3. What strategy were you the least interested in using?

4. What is it about your personality or experience that you believe influenced your lack of interest in that particular strategy?

5. What is one thing you can do now that can help you become more comfortable with the push strategy?

6. The pull strategy?

7. And the move-away strategy?

Questions

When initiating the identifying needs process, there are four types of questions that are very helpful: open-ended, closed-ended, fact, and priority questions.

Open-ended questions encourage customers to share additional information and to expand upon already-stated information. Generally, these cannot be answered with a yes or no. Open-ended questions give customers the control; they can take their responses in whatever direction they choose. Examples include: *Can you give me an idea of how you feel about your advertising? Can you tell me more about that particular need?*

Closed-ended questions only require brief, yes-or-no answers. They are used to limit the customer's response, but when they're overused or used improperly, customers can feel manipulated or shut down during the conversation. Closed-ended questions give the question asker most of the control, which is why they are helpful to define and clarify facts. An example would be: *Does category A need improvement?*

Fact questions allow sales professionals the opportunity to gain objective background information, which can lay the foundation for identifying customers' priorities. Fact-based questions are terrific tools that shed light on a customer's situation, previous experiences, and general areas of concern. Once you understand the background, you have a much better chance of understanding the real need and right solution. But be careful: inexperienced professionals can run into the trap of trying to influence merely with factual information, which can come across as impersonal and generic.

Priority questions encourage customers to provide their subjective feelings, opinions, preferences, priorities, problems, and objectives. Skillfully used, the question-asking process enables the sales professional to separate the trivial from the vital by sifting through many different facets during the course of one meeting. After identifying the real need, you can proceed by exploring other customer concerns and priorities. Your consultative questions may serve a specific purpose or may just be used to move the conversation into varying directions.

The OPEN Model

The image on page 114 shows an overview of the OPEN model, which provides guidance during the identifying needs process. The model is designed to encourage a flow of questions that progresses along a continuum of customer information, from general concerns to specific problems. Questions should emerge naturally as you respect and assess the customer's comfort level.

There is a list here that includes key questions and examples of customer concerns. It's important to remember that each customer experiences problems uniquely, so it's not acceptable to stop once you understand that the customer is concerned about the organization's loyalty. You must go deeper. You must make an effort to see the experience through the customer's eyes.

Types of Questions and Examples

Overview Questions

▷ Tell me about your company's advertising efforts.

▷ How do you execute in-store promotions?

▷ What steps do you take to ensure minimal product waste?

▷ How do you currently train employees on new products?

Problem Questions

▷ What results have your advertising efforts produced?

▷ What sort of responses do your sampling programs generate?

▷ What are your expectations for a supplier?

▷ Last year, what key business objectives did you miss?

▷ This year, what are your success factors?

▷ How do you want us to help you the most?

Elaborate Questions

▷ Can you tell me a bit more about your category reports?

▷ Please explain the decision-making process you referenced.

▷ Can you talk more about your company's campaign to improve its image?

▷ Can you share a few examples of situations when you lost business?

▷ What I hear you saying is that your advertising helps to distinguish your business from your competitors. Is that right?

Need Questions

- ▷ I hear you saying that increased efficiency is your top priority. Am I on track?

- ▷ What impact would it have on your business if we improved this?

- ▷ Bottom line: what are your top two priorities to improve business this year?

- ▷ Your key priority is to provide a cost-effective, high-quality product mix. Is that correct? If we achieved this goal, how would you be affected?

Remember that the identifying needs process is customer-centered, so you should:

- ▷ Transition from general information to more specific, focused information.
- ▷ Earn the right to ask the sensitive questions.
- ▷ Strategically attend to your pace, tone, and sequence matter.
- ▷ Build questions upon each other by preparing plans, reviewing previous discussions, and having a sense of direction.
- ▷ Facilitate a mutual understanding regarding the key objectives by asking questions.
- ▷ Avoid proposing solutions—this is not when they should be introduced.
- ▷ Remember OPEN (Overview, Problem, Elaborate, and Need).

Summary

The identifying needs process may take more than one visit. It will all depend on the customer's needs. Some situations may be complex, requiring a series of meetings to unfold the information gradually; others may be simple and straightforward. The degree of difficulty and depth in this process will vary primarily because each customer is different and each salesperson is different. Some customers may be completely candid about their concerns, whereas others may not even know the root cause of their problem or even be aware of their problem at all. In a case like that, a skilled sales professional may use consultative questions to uncover priorities so that, over a series of sessions, mutual realization can happen. The key steps include asking questions, listening, and raising awareness. All of this must be done skillfully, competently, and effectively.

One of your responsibilities is to help customers discover opportunities they would not have considered, recognized, or pursued without your involvement. Inevitably, this will involve the finances of your business. This is how you deliver value, not only from the products and services you offer, but also from the expertise and experience you possess. If you complete any part of this process without genuine concern, your behavior can appear manipulative or futile. With the right intentions, you won't waste anyone's time.

The final step involves recapping and transitioning the process so that you can request the opportunity to present the suitable solutions. The goal is to effectively summarize and recap in a way that accurately reflects the customer's need from the customer's perspective. This is a complex yet subtle process that separates the amateur salesperson from the Superstar. Beginners often make the all-too-common mistake of discounting prices before they fully understand needs. This approach won't get you anywhere. To be successful and effective, you must:

▷ Master the application of the various types of questions.

▷ Be mindful of the impact different questions and styles have on the customer.

▷ Generate dialogue by using the OPEN model.

▷ Highlight relevant areas of need and opportunity.

▷ Capture the customer's attention by exhibiting genuine intentions.

▷ Initiate and increase the customer's motivation to do business with you.

> *The best product must be sold. People don't come to you and take it away from you. You must go to them.*

> —Edna Newman

Sales Activity Reflection: Identifying Needs

On the left column of the table on the following page, list your customer's key needs. On the right, list specific questions that will help you explore those needs. Remember to consider the OPEN model.

Key Customer Needs	Questions to Explore Those Needs

Presenting Solutions

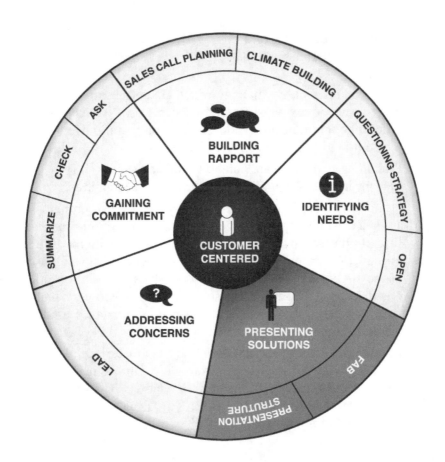

Once you have effectively identified the customer's needs, captured the customer's attention, and expressed the powerful area of opportunity that exists, you are well-positioned to present a solution. Identifying needs is based on listening and understanding, whereas presenting solutions is based on giving. So, when presenting solutions, you must make it a dialogue rather than a monologue. During this step, we will focus on three key areas:

1. Clearly presenting the right product and service solutions.

2. Developing powerful influencing statements.

3. Focusing on the information that was illuminated during the identifying needs step.

The question you want to answer during this stage is this: *How can I best align a solution to meet the customer's needs and priorities?*

Presentation Competencies and FAB

Some of the competencies that are required to effectively present solutions include:

▷ Acting in a persuasive manner, which includes using the influencing techniques we discussed earlier. Also, balancing the different communication modes (push, pull, and move away) is essential to presentation effectiveness.

▷ Presenting in ways that are suitable to both individuals and groups. In many instances, you will need to influence a committee.

▷ Using marketing materials competently will help to compel the audience, while improving the impression the content makes. In fact, the solution itself will be constructed in the FAB format (FAB = features + advantages + benefits). Proper use of the FAB format allows you to describe your solution in a way that directly connects the solution to the customer's high-priority needs. FAB enables you to maintain balance among the different modes of communication.

Features: Features describe or define a characteristic of the product or service. For example: "Our business provides financing for in-store purchases." The feature defines the solution. Features are usually tangible—something you can see, feel, or measure.

Advantages: Advantages describe how the feature works or explains its purpose. An example would be: "The advantage of our financing is that it allows you to find the right option for your financial situation." It's important to note that in order for the feature/advantage to result in a benefit, customers must be able to clearly see how that aspect addresses a high-priority need they have experienced and acknowledged.

Benefits: Benefits explain the value of the product or service to the customer by directly addressing the customer's objectives that were identified during the identifying needs stage. Benefits focus on the outcome and demonstrate how the solution addresses the customer's objectives. For example: "Our performance-driven plan that we discussed will help you combat your competition and increase your revenue."

There are a number of areas that can be adapted using the FAB format, including:

▷ Increased sales.

▷ Better reporting.

▷ Improved customer service.

▷ Increased data credibility.

▷ Upgraded quality.

▷ More convenience.

Feature/Advantage/Benefit statement Areas

▷ Quality.

▷ Products.

▷ Services.

▷ Systems.

▷ Ideas.

▷ Yourself.

▷ Your company.

Feature/Advantage/Benefit statements should be carefully selected and highly customized to meet the specific needs you've identified with your customer. The focus of each statement should be as precise and detailed as possible, while answering the question: *What's in it for me (the customer)?* Benefits can be experienced in various categories and across a wide variety of personal and lifestyle needs.

About Style

A highly focused and well-organized solution is only one element of the salesperson's success. Your style and presence can add a captivating quality to your presentation prescription. Let's face it: we've all been bored by the uninspiring speaker who presents what would otherwise be an effective message. Instead of a stellar speech, the result is a so-so experience.

As you tell the story of your solution, your ability to compel your customers and capture their interest is what separates standard skills from sales success. Pay attention to the style you bring to the solution process. Here are some quick pointers:

▷ Keep your customer engaged. Remember, it's not a monologue; it's about maintaining a dialogue. If you notice customers' eyes glazing over, you can be certain they've lost interest and quit listening. The best way to reengage your customers is to ask questions.

▷ Appropriately balance push, pull, and move away behavior. Maintain an awareness of the impact your presentation is having; if you aren't sure of its impact, the equation to an effective prescription is this: Adjust your style, ask questions, and determine your next push statement.

▷ Distinguish yourself from other professionals by ensuring your style is unique and personalized.

Presentation Process

Effective interpersonal communication and powerful presentations have the following things in common:

▷ Appropriate eye contact and other nonverbal cues.

▷ Voice alterations, tone adjustments, and a positive presence.

▷ Genuine concern and care for the customer.

▷ An interest in listening to the customer.

▷ Excitement regarding the message.

▷ Varying paces to set different cadences to the message at different times.

▷ Authentic and good intentions.

▷ A smile.

Summary

Being your presentation by reinforcing the rapport established. Next, an effective presentation purpose involves aligning your solution to your customer's high-priority needs, creating high-impact influence statements with the FAB format, and developing an engaging style. Also, by using displays and other physical resources, the customer can tangibly interact with the features by seeing, feeling, and touching the product. With discipline and practice, you can significantly improve your presentation delivery and the impact of your solution. Finally, close your presentation by recapping the priorities and focused results while asking for the business, and establishing next steps. Superstar salespeople don't settle for their current level of performance; rather, they consistently look to improve their customer care and sales skills. Use the next two activities to help you achieve a higher level of performance.

> *A man's reach should exceed his grasp, or what's a heaven for?*

—Robert Browning

Sales Activity Reflection: Presenting Solutions—FAB

Identify one of your products and list its FAB. Review this with a peer or manager.

Product Name:		
Feature	Advantage	Benefit
Example: Computer—its large capacity, solid state, hard drive, and memory.	Example: A smaller computer, but a larger memory.	Example: Less space and weight are needed.

Sales Activity Reflection: Demonstration Assessment

At this point, it's important to take some time to review your strengths and areas of improvement. Continually ask yourself: *How can I help my customer more effectively?* Many salespeople do demonstrations as part of their presentations. If this is true for you, rate yourself for how well you do demos using the four characteristics of good demos in this assessment.

Distribute five points in each section. If you cover every area, give yourself a 5. If you miss most of the areas, give yourself a 1.

Name:
Planning: ☐ Organizes material ☐ Understands the demo ☐ Knows how to show the demo
Showing: ☐ Explains the goal, process, and outcome ☐ Shows the customer the product ☐ Reviews how the product works with the customer
Telling: ☐ Remains focused on the customer's needs ☐ Allows the customer to use the product ☐ Is helpful and considerate ☐ Reviews one benefit at a time ☐ Empathizes with the customer
Asking: ☐ Asks the customer for input ☐ Specifically responds ☐ Listens intently ☐ Maintains an appropriate pace ☐ Gains commitment

Strengths:

Areas for Improvement:

The wise man puts himself last and finds himself first.

—Lao Tsu

Cut the Rope That Holds You Back!

Throw a rope around a calf's neck and it's caught. It may struggle and kick to get away, but it can't, because someone else is in control, holding the other end of the rope. Have you ever felt as though you had a rope around your neck? Have you ever felt as though you weren't making any progress in your job? Does it feel as though the rope pulls you back every time you try to move forward? Let's face it: customers complain, sales are missed, your friends don't support you, the competition is rough, your company changes, there are quality problems, and so on. You become frustrated, confused, and tired.

Right and Wrong Forces

In every person there's an odd combination of right and wrong thinking. For the purposes of this message, *right* means what works and *wrong* refers to what doesn't. For every dream, there's darkness; for any ounce of confidence, there's an equal amount of doubt; for every mountain of hope, there's a valley of despair; for every mile of determination, there's the same amount of apathy. Too often, people let the wrong thoughts dominate their thinking, or they let the right thoughts pass by unnoticed. Which pattern will control your life? Which will prevail? Each person experiences this struggle that never ends. Right living is like the game of golf. Hit a few good shots, and you feel great, but once you flub a few, your concentration and confidence slip.

Right living has to be worked at, again and again! In business, there are unlimited opportunities to do well. Yet, many well-intentioned people fall short of their potential. Sometimes the idea of doing business with integrity and providing excellent customer service can seem foreign to people in business, particularly when it comes to applying these principles daily. *It is one thing to talk it, and it's another thing to walk it every day!* Many people's negative habits and poor images from the past stop them in their tracks. Yet there are a few enlightened leaders who are propelled toward success. In spite of obstacles, their vision of professional service is brilliantly executed, which attracts customers and attention from all angles. Think of the salmon that swims upstream every year to spawning waters. The trip is difficult and often fatal, but an inner echo drives them forward to their goal. Isn't every experience in life a possible victory or failure? As Shakespeare said, *it's your choice*: "Nothing is good or bad, except thinking makes it so."

Choose Right Thinking!

Think of a time in your life when you did your best work, closed your largest sale, cared for a friend, laughed hysterically, or romanced your spouse or significant other. How did you feel? How did time pass? You might have been elated, satisfied, happy, and energized. Time most likely passed without notice. Now, think of a time in your life when you did poor work, neglected your friends, cried mournfully, or argued with someone. How did you feel? How did time pass? You might have felt rejected, disgusted, sad, or exhausted. Time most likely moved at a snail's pace. Any of the situations recalled have a number of common characteristics. First, your mind was filled with thoughts about each experience. Second, you experienced feelings. Feelings are just there; they don't need to be good or bad. Third, the passing of time was as constant as the heavens, although you may not have experienced it that way. And fourth, you responded in each experience. *What did you do during and after each experience?* That is the key to success in providing great sales and service and the key to a successful life.

Did you reach up and pull down the best there is to offer, or did you curl up in a ball and let the world push you along? When things didn't work out, you may have focused on the problem and took minor action, if any. But, when things triumphed, you probably envisioned all of the possibilities and let the creativity flow. You had right thoughts about the experience, and then you took action to make positive things happen, rather than lashing out in fear or frustration. What you think, you become! It's always pure choice.

Professionally and personally, your greatest gift is your ability to choose your thoughts and actions. We must do this in good times and bad to be true champions in life. How? Take a break and think, review your goals, remind yourself of your purpose in difficult situations, and remember to focus on the customer's point of view and needs. By learning to think right, you'll do what's right more often. Once you do, you will possess the ability to cut the rope that holds you back from achieving excellence in sales.

Take Right Action!

A prophet was on a hill one day. He told his followers, "I quit." They were aghast and cried out that they needed him; they would do anything for him; they would die for him. The prophet smiled and said, "Live joyously." But the followers put their heads down and walked away slowly. That was too hard to do. All they wanted was to talk and dream about it. If you're not willing to take action, you're no better than the man who starved in a kitchen full of food because he didn't have the sense to cook it.

Our customers define what's right for them. By listening and paying careful attention to them, you'll know the right actions to take. That's the only way to overcome objections, rejection, complaints, and dissatisfaction. Do your work with a smile. Be polite and say thank you. Think innovatively about how you can help customers. Solve problems quickly and kindly. Work cooperatively. Give customers the value they deserve.

You make a difference! You can generate premier results by choosing the right thoughts and actions. A frog once let a scorpion hitch a ride on his back to get across the stream. Somewhere along the way, the scorpion stung the frog. The frog cried, "Why did you do that? Now we'll both drown." The scorpion replied, "I don't know. I guess it's just in my nature." What's your nature? Is it to be tied up, negative about your efforts to sell? Or is it to satisfy customers and do your best? The choice is in your thinking and your actions. Cut the rope that holds you back—*today!*

Sales Activity Reflection: Identify Your Rope

If you don't know what your rope is, it's going to be pretty hard to cut it. So, first things first—identify your rope so that you can take your scissors to it! Don't let it hold onto you anymore. Reflect on your feelings, thoughts, and actions to be freed!

First, read the last few pages again. This time, as you read, answer each question that's asked. Use the space below to journal your answers and thoughts.

Now, really use this space to focus on your *feelings* as they relate to feeling held back.

Now that you know how the rope makes you feel, *identify* your rope(s).

Now that you have an idea of what your rope is and how it makes you feel, list three to five steps or actions you can take in the next week to minimize the rope's grip (if not cut it completely).

How you think when you lose determines how long it will be until you win.

—Gilbert K. Chesterton

Risk vs. Your Rewards

You are about halfway through *Superstar Selling.* It's time to take stock of your efforts.

With almost every element of life, we tend to believe that taking risks is well worth the while. Yes, it's scary, ambiguous, unpredictable, and compromising—*but can we really expect to achieve sales excellence without risking the comfort that comes with complacency?*

That's the question we pose to you today. Think hard and long before you answer. We think it will determine what you do and the direction you head. Therefore, it will define what you achieve.

Think of it like this: When a super-successful person tells you her story, are you more excited about her achievements and her journey if she had to sacrifice a lot to get what she's gotten? Or are you just as stoked when she tells you that everything she has was handed to her? We think we know your answer, if you're anything like the average person. We love a good story that shows a lot of heart, determination, and hard work. Why? Because we admire those people. They inspire us. They remind us of our potential. We all have greatness within us. What are we going to do with it? The answer is this: *We must take risks to reach our truest potential.* Wouldn't you agree?

Professionally and personally, you must break the bounds that hold you back if you want to reap the rewards you long to reach. Here are five of our solutions to stepping outside of our comfort zones:

1. **Do something different daily.**

   Routine removes risk. Doing the same thing over and over builds a degree of comfort that a predictable series of steps will produce an acceptable and expected outcome. At the same time, you can't take advantage of new opportunities unless you open yourself up to the risk of trying something new.

2. **Reflect on how risk-adverse you tend to be.**

   Maintaining an awareness of what you tend to avoid can help you approach unfamiliar territory.

3. **Befriend the brave.**

   Seek out those who approach life the way you want to.

4. **Be patient.**

   Don't expect yourself to be transformed in a week; instead, take minor steps in the direction you hope to head. Before you know it, you'll be looking back on the life you once led, feeling empowered to take on what lies ahead.

5. **Find an accountability partner.**

   The best way to break down the barriers that normally scare you into staying stationary is to tell someone else where you hope to make headway. This person should be someone supportive who can encourage you in your efforts without shaming you when you slip.

Risking comfort and familiarity is hard work, but here's the best news: It's not about what you get in the end; it's about the process of your progress. What you learn, who you become, and all you achieve in the meantime are what really matters. Take it from someone who did the impossible—Amelia Earhart, who said, "The most difficult thing is the decision to act, the rest is merely tenacity. The fears are paper tigers. You can do anything you decide to do. You can act to change and control your life; and the procedure, the process is its own reward."[1] Now that's a Superstar attitude and approach.

Now, answer this: *How do you move toward the greatest risks that hold the greatest rewards?*

> *To speak and to speak well are two things. A fool may talk,*
> *but a wise man speaks.*
>
> —Ben Jonson

Sales Activity Reflection: Risk vs. Your Reward

Describe your daily routine. How can you improve it to be more productive?

What risks have you taken recently in your sales approach? What happened? What can you learn?

What risks have you been avoiding? What are you losing? What could you gain?

Whom can you talk to who is supportive, who will give you perspective that you need to break through and help hold you accountable (besides your boss or spouse)?

Addressing Customer Concerns

Oftentimes, salespeople can set the tone for their own success by handling customer objections and concerns professionally. Research indicates that 80 percent of sales are made after the fifth point of contact; however, 80 percent of salespeople quit trying after the first or second attempt.[1] So, despite challenges they might face, Superstar salespeople continue to give themselves another chance for the business. The number-one reason salespeople fear objection is because they lack problem-solving skills, so they avoid confrontational situations, quit too early, and derail their sales success.

So what are the objections you receive from customers?

▷ The price?

▷ The quality?

▷ The technology?

▷ The responsiveness of customer service?

▷ The customer doesn't need or want the offer?

▷ The customer is happy with his/her current product or service?

▷ The customer wants to think about it?

▷ The customer needs to talk to a manager or group?

▷ Other? (Name it.)

Remember, selling wouldn't be all that hard without objections, right? True! Without customer concerns, you would be an order taker; in that case, anyone could do your job. Resistance means you're approaching the real matters, where the rubber meets the road. It takes a professional to engage the customer on these issues. That's why selling is considered the lowest-paying easy work and the highest-paying hard work. The sooner you get to the objections, the closer you are to the sale.

You are a sales professional. Professionals understand the dynamics of making a decision for a customer. Sometimes, what customers actually object to and what they say they object to are two different things. Most of the time, it's the fear of making a decision that drives customers to delay saying yes to a sales professional. This is why common concerns are: *It will cost too much, I have to think it over, I need to see if we have room in the budget,* and *I think your product is more than we need.* The key question for you to solve this issue is this: *How can I positively deal with customer resistance?*

The sales process is not a contest, a battle, or even a game; it's not a win-or-lose scenario. Obviously, it could be if you don't care about your potential customers. It's really a relationship-building process, and your goal is to help your customers solve problems, meet needs, and enjoy satisfying and successful lives. Superstar selling is about creating win-win relationships through integrity, positive performance, and genuine care and trust, in order to form profitable and mutually beneficial long-term partnerships. Anyone can sell something once. A professional can sell the same product repeatedly to loyal customers, while turning current customers into great references for future business opportunities.

The LEAD Model

So how do you address customer concerns? First, you need to change objections into concerns, as the previous perspective demonstrated. When someone objects, he/she is building barriers or opposing views; when someone has a concern, he/she needs help with an issue. That's where the Superstar selling process intersects with the LEAD Model. There are four key ingredients to the model:

▷ **Listen.** Are you really customer-centered?

▷ **Explore.** Do you know what the customer is trying to communicate?

▷ **Attend.** Are your attitude and behavior demonstrating that you care?

▷ **Deliver a solution.** Do you have a customized solution that addresses the customer's needs?

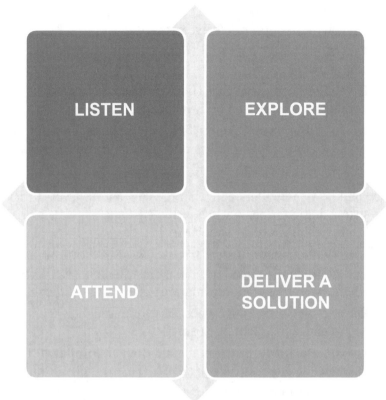

Sales professionals seek out concerns by checking in periodically during the sales process instead of waiting until the end of their sales presentation for the inevitable objection. It's about understanding the customer's position in the buying process: interest, clarity of concerns, learning and analysis, evaluation, and decision-making. A customer-centered focus ensures that you understand the following: *Are we on track? Do you have questions so far? And does this make sense or seem helpful?*

As you experience reactions, clarify misunderstandings, defuse emotions in difficult areas, handle objections, and resolve differences that emerge, are you accurately and appropriately addressing concerns by maintaining an open dialogue?

Listen

Are you really customer-centered? Your goal is to focus on the customer's needs and objectives, rather than your need for a sale or a quick resolution. This is a pull process to understand the concern and to extract your level of engagement.

1. Do you want to listen?
2. Do you make appropriate eye contact?
3. Do you use verbal cues (for example: *yes, I see, okay, I understand*)?
4. Do you use nonverbal cues (for example: taking notes, nodding, using relevant body language)?
5. Do you paraphrase or summarize your understanding of the issue (for example: *If I understand you correctly, you mean...*)?

Explore

Do you know and understand what the customer is trying to say? Use questions to gain better perspective of the customer's point of view. This could include pull or move away behavior.

1. Do you maintain your composure and act professionally?
2. Do you ask open-ended questions (for example: what, how, where, why) to gather information?
3. Do you use closed-ended questions (requiring only a yes or a no) to gain agreement or closure?
4. Do you use directives to obtain additional information (for example: *Tell me more about that*)?
5. Do you paraphrase for understanding?

Attend

Is your attitude communicating that you care? Positive pull communication is a result of three things:[2]

Words: Use constructive, conversational, and non-confrontational language; this equals 7 percent of your communication's impact.

Tone of voice: Maintain a similar volume and tone of voice as the customer; this equals 38 percent of your communication's influence.

Physiology: Ensure that your actions and body language are congruent with a real desire to be of service; this equals 55 percent of your communicative power.

1. Do you maintain your focus on the customer by withholding your response until you have gained an accurate and complete understanding?

2. Do you pay attention to the customer's demeanor and emotions?

3. If needed, do you ask further clarifying questions?

Deliver a Solution

Do you have a customized solution that is customer-centered? In other words, are you ready to respond based on understanding the customer's perspective of the situation or problem? This is push behavior.

1. Do you summarize your understanding?

2. Do you specifically respond?

3. Do you seek agreement on the issue, address next steps, and ask for the business?

The LEAD model includes a balanced understanding and an appropriate presentation of your product solution. But, it begins by understanding: listen, explore, and attend. This will decrease the customer's resistance because it allows you and your customer the chance to unpack emotional responses constructively. Finally, it ensures a focused response that's more likely to address the customer's actual concerns. The LEAD model is visually represented here. You'll notice that the process is iterative, with repetitive *listen, explore,* and *attend* steps. This is to ensure that the customer's concern is correctly identified before attempting to deliver the solution.

Using the LEAD Model: Examples

SP = sales professional

C = customer

Example #1: I think I can get along a little longer with my current vendor.

SP:	It sounds like you have a concern about making a change? Can you tell me about it?	Listen—Explore
C:	Yes, I'm just not sure it's worth it to make the switch.	
SP:	Can you tell me more about what you mean by "worth it"?	Attend—Listen—Explore
C:	This seems so complicated—so hard. I just don't know if it's worth it for me to go through all the bother and effort to switch.	

SP:	It sounds like you're concerned about whether the value of our service outweighs the effort to change your process, so you're questioning whether it makes sense to switch. Is that right?	Attend—Listen—Explore
C:	Yes, that's exactly how I feel.	
SP:	Is there anything in particular that you're concerned about, as it relates to your service we've been discussing?	Explore
C:	I'm afraid we won't be a priority, and that it will be too pricy.	
SP:	You're concerned that you won't be able to afford the change, and that you won't be important to us. Is that correct?	Attend—Listen
C:	Yes.	
SP:	That's why I'm here to help. We have an array of options to ensure the transition happens as efficiently and effortlessly as possible. Also, with the size of our distribution network, all of our customers are a priority. Why don't we review the process and some affordable options, so that I can get you what you need in a timely manner?	Attend—Deliver a Solution
C:	Yes, that sounds good. Let's do it!	

Example #2: Your price is too high.

SP:	Ms. Jones, usually when customers are concerned about prices, they are questioning the value of the product or they're concerned about their budget. Can you share a bit more about your pricing concerns with me?	Listen—Explore—Attend
C:	I know I can get the product at a better margin than you are offering.	

SP:	So, your prices from another supplier give you a better margin. Is that what you are saying?	Attend—Listen—Explore
C:	Yes, I've talked to the competition, and they can beat your price.	
SP:	So, you have a proposal from them that is guaranteed and comparable to the parameters I recommended?	Attend—Listen—Explore
C:	Not yet, but their price is 10–15 percent better in the long term than your offer.	
SP:	Based on initial discussions, I can understand how you might think our price is high. We're aware of the other supplier's offer and emphasis on price. We want to provide you the right product mix to meet your needs and to help you build a profitable and successful business over time. If you'll work with us, we'll carefully determine a business plan that's right for you. We're confident that you'll find our price to be very competitive, and, even more importantly, we're convinced that our plan will help you meet your customers' needs more effectively. May we proceed on that basis?	Attend—Deliver a Solution—Explore
C:	Sure. But, I still need a great price.	
SP:	Great. May I ask you a few more questions to determine what the best options are?	Attend—Explore
C:	Yes.	

LEAD Assessment

Rate yourself on a scale of 1–5 based on how you handle objections. What do you do well? Where do you need to improve? Ask your manager to observe one of your sales calls, and then request feedback on how you handled objections. The form on the following page can be used to record the feedback.

Listen:
  ___ Wants to listen
  ___ Makes eye contact
  ___ Uses verbal cues
  ___ Uses nonverbal gestures
  ___ Paraphrases the concern

Explore:
  ___ Maintains professionalism and composure
  ___ Uses open-ended questions to understand
  ___ Uses closed-ended questions to focus
  ___ Uses directives to gather more information
  ___ Paraphrases again, if appropriate

Attend:
  ____Remains focused on the customer's needs
  ____Pays attention to the customer's demeanor
  ____Asks additional clarifying questions if needed

Deliver a Solution:
  ____Summarizes understanding of the concern
  ____Specifically responds
  ____Asks for the sale

Strengths	Areas to Improve

I wish people who have trouble communicating would just shut up.

—Tom Lehrer

Sales Activity Reflection: Objectify Your Objections

So, if you've been a sales professional for more than a day, the chances you've been given an objection are greater than the chances you've made a sale. That's just the reality of sales. That's not meant to discourage you; it's meant to normalize the selling environment, so that you don't take things personally when it's not always about you.

Objections have great potential because once we understand why we're getting them, what kind we're receiving, and how we're reacting to them, we can develop strategies to respond more effectively and professionally. Answer these next few questions to look at your objections objectively.

1. List five objections that you have received at one point or another (ideally, you would list the most common objections you hear).
2. How do you feel when you're given an objection? List at least two or three emotions.
3. On a scale of 1–5 (1 = highly unlikely; 5 = highly likely), how likely is it that your customer knows your feelings (in Question 2)?
4. What do you think when you're given an objection? List two to three thoughts that come to mind in that moment.
5. On a scale of 1–5 (1 = never; 5 = always), how often do you share your thoughts with your customer (in Question 4)?

6. If you have a hard time keeping your thoughts or feelings from your client, what is one thing you believe you can start doing now to minimize what "seeps through" during the sales process?

7. In your opinion, is there any benefit to sharing your feelings and thoughts with your customer(s)? If so, list the benefits you believe exist.

8. When reviewing your answers to Question 1, brainstorm a list of reasons that your customers could have when raising the objections they do. In other words, dig deep into the reasons behind their objections. Why might they be saying what they are saying?

9. After making a list of possibilities in Question 8, do most reasons involve you?

10. In this space, document any thoughts you have after completing this exercise.

Overcoming Sales Resistance

If you're in sales, you know that challenges and objections are part of the gig. How a salesperson responds to such hiccups says a lot about that particular sales representative.

There's a saying that goes something like this: "The difference between stumbling blocks and stepping stones is how you use them." We love this quote because it helps us change the way we view opposition.

What we find fascinating is that everyone in sales knows that resistance is inevitable, yet most sales professionals believe they ought to be an exception to the rule, so when they experience opposition they take it personally. This is the most serious mistake a salesperson can make when confronting a client's skepticism. Regardless of how great you are at sales, it's ignorant to think you're an exception to any rule. The best people in sales don't make it about them; they make it about their clients. You can't predict how your clients will respond, you can't control their challenges, and you can't avoid their hard questions. So, instead of being shut down by it all, you have the opportunity to use these moments as milestones.

Here are five tips for keeping it cool when put under fire by a customer:

1. **Remain open. Don't get defensive.**
   Again, don't take things personally. If you are able to make it about their challenge instead of making it about yourself, you will have a much better chance of continuing the conversation and affirming the client's concerns. This is essential if you hope to establish a credible relationship.

2. **Maintain curiosity. Ask questions.**

   If your clients are apprehensive about something you're trying to sell, ask more questions to really get to the root of their worry. Acknowledging that you want to fully address their concerns can work wonders.

3. **Seek to understand. Don't strive to explain**.

   Too often, when sales reps are challenged they get flustered and jump into explanatory mode, hoping that by sharing more information, the client will feel more secure. But throwing more information at a client is pointless if you don't accurately understand his or her real concerns.

4. **Be patient and professional.**

   If you go into the conversation with one goal—to sell x, y, or z to the client—and you are challenged, you will get frustrated that your goal wasn't accomplished. The key is to make it about the customer from the get-go. Your goal should be to solidify a relationship with the customer, so that you can meet his or her needs as time progresses. If you're pushy about your product, you'll end up pushing your client away.

5. **Stay present. Don't give up or get grumpy.**

   If you're facing resistance, it can be easy to shut down, walk away, or give up on the customer altogether. Don't. This requires resilience, and your client will respect your willingness to walk through the hard stuff. As Duke Ellington said, "A problem is a chance to do your best."

Sales Activity Reflection: Overcoming Sales Resistance

Answer the following questions about how you handle sales objections or resistance:

1. Describe the toughest objection you've received lately.
2. What was it and how did it make you feel?
3. What can you learn from this day's lesson that might have helped you?
4. What do you do well in handling resistance?
5. What do you want to improve even more?

The Secret Sauce of Selling

Are you in sales? Great! Think back to previous conversations you've had with your clients. Think back to the first five minutes of your first customer interaction. What was it about? Chances are, the conversation revolved around *you*. If that's the truth, own up to it. And now, change it.

You probably spewed out your experience, your company's story, your products, your services, your other clients, your success, the awards you've won, the accomplishments you've achieved, and so on—you know, all that impressive, interesting information that nobody really wants to hear, except *you*.

Your customer really couldn't care less about this stuff (initially). Another time, another day—when a relationship has been built—you can share these fascinating little facts. But, during this first interaction, it is critical to focus on your customer. The easiest way to hit this argument home is to put yourself in any other setting. Anytime you meet new people, if they go on and on about themselves, you probably lose interest immediately and leave the conversation convinced their ego is reason enough to avoid them in the future.

If you started rambling about yourself, your story, your experience, your skills, and your success, they'd internally roll their eyes and silently redirect attention. Why do sales professionals seem to think the same doesn't apply to them when they are selling?

Your customers want the focus—all of it—to be on them, their needs, and their story. So make it that way. Here are a few suggestions on how to make it more about them and less about you:

▷ Ask questions.

▷ Explain your reasons for wanting to talk with them.

▷ Share a story that would be meaningful to them.

▷ Understand before you explore.

▷ Explicitly explore their needs and expectations.

▷ Only make promises when you can commit to fulfilling them.

▷ Give them something that will give them a taste of what you're selling.

▷ Make specific statements; avoid ambiguous or blanket statements.

▷ Do your research. (It shows that you respect their time.)

▷ Be original; do something in that first sales interaction that will leave them with a good first impression.

▷ Close the conversation with a follow-up clincher. (You don't want them wondering what to expect.)

Put your clients first. Everybody wants to be prioritized. So make it about them when it matters, and hopefully they'll return the favor by making it about you when a decision needs to be made. Do it authentically, and do it genuinely. Selfless sales is the secret to sales success.

Sales Activity Reflection: The Secret Sauce of Selling

Answer the following questions as you review how your sales approach has changed since you started this book:

1. What have you learned or relearned so far?
2. What can you do to be even more customer-focused?
3. Where have you made the most improvement?
4. What do you want to improve even more?
5. Describe one success story you have had using the concepts of Superstar selling.

Closing the Sale

When closing the sale, the key question is this: *How can I help my customer make the right decision that addresses his or her needs and priorities?* You do that by presenting product benefits, providing appropriate pricing options, guiding the customer to an understanding of the solution, reviewing the key elements of a solution, and asking for the sale.

If you want your sales to grow, you need to summarize the needs and product benefits, gain agreement, and ask for the business! Some salespeople are reluctant to close a sale or offer specific solutions. That's not surprising—for a couple of reasons:

▷ **People are taught not to ask for what they want.** Instead, they're supposed to wait for an offer, direction, or an inspiration. Being direct is often looked at as being pushy or insensitive. But when appropriate, *it's important to ask.* The customer knows why you are there; if you leave him or her wondering, you create unnecessary pressure.

▷ **People fear rejection.** It's like asking someone on a date and getting turned down. Who wants that sort of pain or embarrassment? Salespeople often worry that if they present specific solutions, the customer will offer an objection or say no.

▷ **Some people are too direct.** We remember buying a company car. After meeting the salesperson, we were asked five times before he knew our names, "If I can find the car you want at an affordable price, will you buy today?" Talk about skipping all the sales steps. Or, did you ever get a call from someone selling stock? After 30 seconds you're asked to invest $25,000 in a hot product, right now. This blunt approach builds no rapport and yields few sales.

Yet, unless you present a solution and ask for the sale, you'll never know what the customer thinks. Presenting and closing gives customers the chance to improve their business by saying yes to the opportunity that meets their need. Objections imply that the customer needs more information to proceed or has a concern that needs to be addressed.

Although there are a number of best-selling books that teach selling techniques, all of that advice isn't necessary. Sales professionals don't need to wear extravagant clothes to sell effectively; they simply need a genuine desire and honest attitude to be of service. You need to help your customers meet their needs, solve their problems, and feel good about the business solutions you're proposing. If you tenaciously follow the Superstar selling model and remain customer-centered, these four steps will help you close sales so that you can gain the business—again and again:

1. **Present product benefits.** You are a trained professional. If you have worked closely with the customer, you know the right solution that addresses his or her needs.

2. **Offer options.** When multiple options can meet the customer's needs, be sure to offer all alternatives so that the customer can consider which he or she prefers.

3. **Review.** Evaluate the information you have gathered about the customer in order to come to the right solution.

4. **Ask Confidently.** Close your sales boldly, because you have worked hard to know and understand what will help the customer. If you approach the solution tentatively, the customer will see your uncertainty as doubt, which may force him or her to question your recommendation. Here are four ways to ask:

   ▷ Action Close: *Can I get your approval?*

   ▷ Assumptive Close: *When do you want it delivered?*

   ▷ Alternative Close: *Do you want 50 or 100 sets to start?*

   ▷ Added Step Close: *Let's schedule our kickoff in two weeks. What works for you?*

Steps to Close the Sale

Effectively selling and closing is a process more than it is a single act of influencing, which is why so many sales professionals aren't good at it. It begins before the initial meeting, continues during the identifying needs stage, and requires superb follow-up service and care.

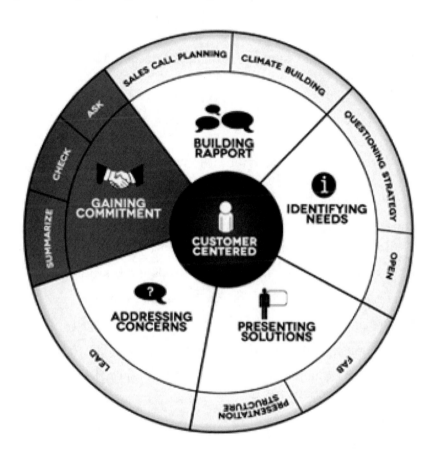

▷ What can you do to better prepare the customer to make a commitment?

▷ What shortcuts do you take? How can you avoid taking them?

▷ What will you do today to improve your closing ratios?

Use this checklist for better closing and increased sales success!

1. Before the Sale: Prepare

   ▷ Understand communication preferences and personality styles of customers.

   ▷ Prepare for potential questions or objections.

   ▷ Arrange your tools, samples, and materials so that they are ready and accessible.

   ▷ Remember that your goal is to meet a need and solve a problem.

   ▷ Know the FAB of your solution.

   ▷ Practice different closing approaches.

   ▷ Mentally rehearse a successful sale.

   ▷ Thoroughly understand the customer and her market: Website review, company market data, possible referral information, financial analysis, and so forth.

2. During the Sale: Follow the Superstar Selling Model

   ▷ Take the time to build trust and rapport.

   ▷ Ask probing questions to identify needs and priorities.

   ▷ Listen carefully and summarize by paraphrasing.

   ▷ Present your solution benefits effectively and honestly.

   ▷ Demonstrate your product. Help the customer buy wisely.

   ▷ Avoid judgmental or defensive behavior, especially when addressing concerns.

   ▷ Use LEAD.

   ▷ Ask for the sale!

3. After the Sale: Follow Up

   ▷ Check that you and your customer are in agreement on the idea.

   ▷ Follow up in a number of ways at different times. Examples include thank-you notes, letters, phone calls, e-mails, and personal contacts. Satisfied customers will give you more business and refer other business your way.

   ▷ Deal with problems directly, promptly, and professionally.

▷ Keep your commitments. If you can't, call, explain, and reschedule.

▷ Ask for referrals.

▷ Continue to add value through newsletters, consumer and industry information, new ideas, personal interest, and the unexpected recognition.

Closing Success

Our experience indicates that if you do an excellent job during the sales process, as we have discussed in each aspect of the Superstar selling process, 50 percent of customers will ask you how they can buy the product. Essentially, they will close their own sale. Sales professionals just need to follow through. And when customers don't close their own sale, salespeople need to ask for the order. Yet, our research still shows that salespeople ask only about 10 percent of the time. Can you believe that? With all the work it takes to secure a customer opportunity, salespeople still don't ask. Instead, they say things such as:

▷ *Do you have any questions?*

▷ *Do you have my card?*

▷ *Do you understand the features?*

▷ *Can I give you some additional resources?*

▷ *You may want to look us up on the Internet.*

▷ *If you're interested, just give me a call.*

▷ *Oh, um, let me know if you need anything else.*

Too many salespeople dance around the issue of asking for a commitment. One professional consultant who worked with us just couldn't look someone in the eyes and ask for the sale, yet he was good at every other step of the process. Why don't more salespeople do this? It's fear—fear of rejection, resistance, and even success. It's very similar to what we discussed when addressing customer concerns and objections. Remember the LEAD model when closing. Closing is about the ability to guide someone to a decision. The entire Superstar sales process centers on understanding how to help a customer and then gaining a customer's commitment-closing. That's the goal!

4 Key Closes

With preparation, practice, and perseverance, you can learn to close more effectively. We recommend that during sales-call planning, reps write out two sales-closing statements they could use. This forces them to think through in advance what they will do. We don't believe you need 1,001 ways to close a sale. This is especially true if you follow the Superstar sales process. First, as mentioned, many customers close themselves. Second, if you plan in advance, you are more focused. Third, with the Superstar selling process, you are building commitment—closing—each step of the way. Because you are building commitment along the way, try these four closes and watch your success soar.

Action Close

The Action Close is simple and straightforward in asking for the business: *Can I have your approval, right here?* or *May I have your approval please?* We recommend you don't say "signature," because it is so formal and contractual. It scares some customers into delaying a decision. In one situation, we went through a six-month process of identifying needs, planning, and presenting. The proposal and solution were right on. The key decision-maker said, "Let's do it." Then he walked out the door. Rick jumped up and said, "I need just a minute." He and the decision-maker went in a small room and Rick closed officially by saying, "I need your approval—here." The decision-maker signed, they shook hands, and—boom!—it was done.

Alternative Close

This is where you give the customer a choice of options: *We can do delivery Tuesday or Thursday. Which do you prefer?* or *What color do you want: red or black?* Customers like choices; it gives them a feeling of control. You can give customers choices in color, size, model, total numbers, dates, times, product options, warranties, and many other things. Always be up-front and get their signature on your paperwork.

Assumptive Close

With the Assumptive Close, you act as if you had an agreement already. Use this agreement as a base during your other sales steps. You gain their agreement on a next-level issue that means that the customer accepts your proposal. For example: *When do you want delivery?* or *Who do you want on the steering committee?* or *Where will you put it?*

Added Step Close

Sometimes, no matter what you do, customers won't decide today. In many cases they need time to crunch their numbers or to talk to other parties. Many times their lawyers need to look at the proposal and contract. You can close nearly 100 percent of the time with the Added Step Close. Your goal is to establish a definitive next step for final closure. For example: *You said it would take two weeks for the review. Let's set a date to finalize everything. What would work for you in this time frame?* Here's another example: *Let's establish a next meeting to review the details. What is good for you next week?* You can always use this close to move the sales process forward.

Sales Activity Reflection: Gaining Commitment

Answer the following questions: *What are you doing well? How can you improve?*

1. Why do many sales professionals avoid saying the words that close the sale?
2. What mistakes do sales professionals often make in gaining commitment?
3. What must sales professionals do better to close more effectively?
4. What does the following quote mean? "Don't oversell. If you do, it's like knocking on a turtle shell trying to get him to stick his head out."

5 Ways to Increase Sales Today

How can you increase sales today? That's a challenge we hear frequently from sales management. If you have a competitive product, your only limitation is creative thinking. Here's a story that illustrates this point. Einstein taught at Princeton University for 22 years. Every night the janitor who cleaned his classroom found the blackboard filled with complex equations. At the bottom of the blackboard was the word "erase." In the upper-right-hand corner of the blackboard Einstein always wrote: $1 + 1 = 2$. Below that was written "save." Intellectuals have theorized that Einstein favored the creative mind, but always encouraged everyone to begin with the basics. That's good thinking for improving sales, too! Take a few minutes and talk to the top sales rep at any company. You'll quickly learn there are some key things he or she does better than others. You could literally double and triple your commission checks! (We are talking about thousands of dollars here.) If you want to make more money and enjoy more success and recognition, pay close attention.

Talk to More Qualified Prospects or Customers

Before you call a customer, warm him or her up with a series of added-value e-mails. Through surveys of top-selling sales reps in Canada and the United States, we found they meet with five customers or prospects a day. We call it the "5 Plan." (Some even do a "sales blitz" talk to a whole week's worth of customers in one day!) Quite frankly, as a rule, the best sales individuals in any company have more customer contacts. In order to sell a lot you need to proactively talk to customers about their needs and your products. Start today. Focus and create a specific plan. You will begin to see results in as soon as one week. Within a month you will experience even better results!

Set and Track Your Goals

Your managers already do this. However, you have to do it for yourself, too. The best performers in any industry are meticulous about how much money they want to make, what they will do with the money, and where they are at any moment with respect to those goals. Goal setting helps you become a meaningful specific, and not a wandering generality. Your personal goals give you the motivation to act and to do it with a sense of urgency. Wow! We have talked about knowing your numbers, and we will work on goals in more detail in the coming sections.

Keep Learning

Top professionals in any field keep learning and training. In basketball a computer program was set up to identify the top five superstars of all time. The computer looked at scoring, rebounds, championships, assists, years in the league, and so forth. Who do you think was number one? Doctor J was number five. Larry Bird came in at number four. Wilt Chamberlain was number three. Magic Johnson was number two. Michael Jordan was number one![1]

Each player had a short bio describing his accomplishments. Each mentioned the person's dedication to training to stay at the top of his game! It's been said in sales that if you increase your learning, you will increase your earning. Why not commit yourself to serious study? If you increase your learning you will increase your earning.

Follow Up

The greatest closing technique of all time is follow-up. Most people in sales positions or services that sell as part of their jobs stop short. They give up too easily. As we've mentioned previously, 80 percent of all sales come after five or more attempts. Use a customer relationship management system to track needed follow-up. You will have far too many prospects and customers to remember all that must be done. Besides, opportunities will slip through. Get organized, and your income will increase.

Believe in Yourself

This isn't a motivational speech. It is a reminder to focus on your strengths. It is a reminder that you have tremendous potential. You are like a tiny acorn that has the pattern of mighty oak tree. We are not talking about self-improvement, either. This is not self-improvement; this is only increasing your ability to be all that you already are. Dig deeper and use the talent you already have. If you have to mine it, ask for some training or coaching. Take a college course or two. Two of the best ways to believe in yourself are to help others and spread good news through a positive attitude. It's amazing how this will help you, too. It's like a mirror affect. William Clement Stone once said, "If you can conceive it, if you can believe it, you can achieve it!" That's what Superstar selling is all about!

Sales Activity Reflection: 5 Ways to Increase Sales Today

Answer the following questions about your recent sales activity:
• Think about the last month. What three or four things are you doing well in your sales activities?
• What have you learned or relearned from your customers and prospects?
• What do you want to do differently or better next month?

The Greatest Closing Technique of All Time

Did you know that 70–80 percent of all projects fail because they are lacking follow-up or follow-through?[1]

It's true. This means that all of the pre-work is planned and executed—and then all of that hard work gets tossed into the trash. It's all for nothing without proper follow-up and follow-through. That happens to many, many sales as well.

Imagine this: You walk into a restaurant. The host seats you and your family. You are given menus to review the choices. You see the cooks in the kitchen, preparing something scrumptious. You can smell the delicious dishes. You have silverware, a glass, a plate, and a napkin. But, your server forgets to follow up. You didn't even have a chance to order. You're let down before you even taste the famous food. Or, less dramatically, the server forgets the dessert you ordered, and you wait extraordinarily long for the check. In other words, the restaurant's food reputation means nothing to you because nobody follows through. It's too late for whatever is supposedly so great.

Whether you're the one doing business or you're the business looking for help, remember that skirting around these two steps means you're further from achieving your success. Follow up and follow through to do what most forget to do. It's the greatest closing technique of all time. Why? It means:

1. Following through on your commitments.

2. Over-promising and over-delivering.

3. Bringing up added value to the customer.

4. Going the extra mile.

5. Replying to requests, e-mails, or phone calls in a timely and thorough manner.

6. Handling complaints completely and professionally.

7. Keeping in touch through calls, e-mails, letters, newsletters, and so forth.

8. Expressing appreciation to the customer with creative ways to say thank you.

9. Providing a customer survey for feedback.

10. Bringing up other products or options to help the customer.

11. Delivering education or training to our customer on using your products.

Early in our business we learned a valuable lesson about follow-up. It was in the summer months, and business was a little slower than normal for that time of the year. We did a marketing campaign for our customers that included a newsletter and an appreciation phone call. Within a month we had business from 70 percent of them.

Sales Activity Reflection: The Greatest Closing Technique of All Time

How do you follow up with your accounts now?

What four to five things will you do to improve?

Success Practices and Peak Performance

Your Mental Models

Over nine decades ago, Dr. Evan O'Neill Kane of New York's Kane Summit Hospital felt doctors were losing too many patients during appendectomy surgery, many because of the effects of general anesthesia. He felt that local anesthesia would be better for the patient but, not surprisingly, no volunteers opted to test his hypothesis—until February 15, 1921. That's when he finally performed an appendectomy with local anesthesia—on himself! During the procedure, he changed the way this surgery was practiced in medicine.[1] To be your best, you often need to change, too; sometimes that change requires operating on yourself! Begin analyzing your mentality by counting how many times the letter *F* appears.

> FEATURE FILMS ARE THE RE-
>
> SULT OF YEARS OF SCIENTI-
>
> FIC OF STUDY COMBINED WITH THE
>
> FORMAL EXPERIENCE OF YEARS

How many did you get? Four? Five? Six? Seven? There are eight! If you missed any, why did you? Why would anyone miss an *F* or two or three? It has to do with our mental model, or the way we perceive things and act on them. This little exercise illustrates that what you are missing in terms of performance improvement is most likely right in front of you.

Sometimes the solutions to your challenges are there, but you just don't see them. Why? Because of deep-rooted habits, perceptions, and beliefs. In fact, when you make efforts to improve, it can seem as futile as trying to lose weight with fad diets.

So what's the key? How do you break through? Dr. Charles Garfield of the Peak Performance Institute has discovered exercises that help individuals reach their personal best performance levels. Garfield experienced these techniques himself as a world-class weight lifter and researcher. Garfield explains, "In the process, the researchers discovered that mental training techniques not only combated negative reactions, but also threw open the doors to hidden reserves of energy and endurance."[2] In his own work with Olympic athletes and businesspeople, Dr. Denis Waitley found similar peak-performance strategies of superstars.[3] To begin, remember these important principles:

▷ **Self-development is self-management.** There is no self-improvement; it's about increasing your ability to be all that you already are. You can't change others, but you can change yourself.

▷ If you hope to sell more effectively by managing yourself, **you must be willing to change some habits** to increase your productivity.

▷ A basic self-management principle is to **respond to all events based on your goals and priorities,** rather than reacting to spot urgencies, problems, or needs.

▷ The mind and body are intertwined: To control what you do, **work on controlling what you think.**

Just as a champion systematically, physically, and mentally prepares to win the gold in the Olympics, Superstar salespeople do the same. Know your product, learn selling techniques, become customer-centered, and prepare yourself mentally to handle setbacks. We call it *emotional resiliency.* During the next few days you will be challenged to expand your comfort zone. The activities presented in Day 22 through Day 26 will help you to take much of what you've learned and apply it to the next steps in your sales development and sales career. You will learn success practices that will inspire you to Superstar selling excellence.

Sales Activity Reflection: Self-Management and Resiliency

Before starting the next few sales activities, it's time for some self-reflection. You can't fully comprehend all you can be if you don't know what you think about yourself now. Are you prepared to take a peek into your perspective on your potential? Rate yourself 1–5 (1 = not true at all; 5 = very true) on each of the questions. Be honest about what you currently believe about yourself.

1.		I think good things about myself most of the time.
2.		I am open to feedback, even if it's constructive.
3.		My feelings and my thoughts are typically congruent.
4.		I tend to do what I think I should do; I am consistent.
5.		I know I have more potential than I'm using right now.
6.		I get disappointed on occasion, but eventually I regain my confidence.
7.		It's easy for me to see the positive in a situation.
8.		When I'm not feeling at my best, I do whatever it takes to get there!
9.		I look at what I can do differently before I look at the faults of others.
10.		I tend to respond more than I react.

Review your answers. The higher your answers, the more positive you are about who you are, what you offer, and the potential you have. The lower your answers, the more time and attention you might need to give to develop a more positive self-image. How you think about yourself and your abilities will inherently affect your interactions with customers, your reactions to objections, and your resiliency over time.

Mentally, you have the potential to model your best. It's up to you!

Best of the Best Exercise

Think of a time during your sales career when you did your best work. Choose a situation that exemplifies your highest performance. Get a clear mental picture of the event. Replay it in your mind as though it were a movie. Think of the details: the people, problems, sounds, feelings, and surroundings. Mentally review what happened, how you behaved, and what you felt and achieved. Be as specific as possible in terms the actions you took to capture the customer's trust, identify needs, present a compelling solution, and close the sale with confidence. Note your feelings of accomplishment and what the customer and your coworkers said to you. Capture your thoughts in the space below.

Briefly describe the situation:

What was your motivation to succeed or act?
How did you feel?
What key behaviors or strategies did you use?
What lessons can you learn or relearn from your peak performance experience?

By learning to replicate that experience and improving the results, you'll become a sales leader. To be the best you can be, make a commitment to personal development and excellence. If you want to be exceptional, do exceptional things. The difference between sales winners and losers is that the winners do what losers won't do. Never forget that success is not accidental. Success momentum is achieved by reviewing what we do right and then learning to apply it consciously, through deliberate thought and action. It's how you learn to sell "in the zone." It's the place elite athletes go when endeavoring to deliver their best performances in the heat of competition. The next days will reinforce this concept in your sales behavior.

Goal Achievement

The best salespeople are goal achievers. They are meticulous about their numbers and what they have to do to achieve them. Goals become realities when you act on them; therefore, nothing great in sales has ever been achieved without action. "The great end in life is not knowledge, but action," declared British educator and biologist Thomas Henry Huxley. Goals are the motivators behind your actions. When you are discouraged or disappointed, review your goals to remind yourself of who you are, what you want, and what you are becoming. Remind yourself what you have to gain by taking action and what you will lose if you don't.

Effective goal achievement involves writing a specific and realistic goal. Then, you must separate the goal into smaller steps on which you can take action. The first step is the most important because it's where you start. Many goals are unachieved because people fail to begin. Remember, the journey of a thousand miles begins with the first step. And then, follow through. Just as you wouldn't start a car and expect to go anywhere without putting it in gear, you shouldn't expect your goals to be achieved without taking action.

Finally, successful goal achievement includes reviewing your progress. People rarely grow from experience because they don't choose to learn from it. After each action you take, you must evaluate the results. In summary, close the GAP on goal success by:

G—writing the **g**oal.

A—establishing **a**ction steps.

P—**p**roactively reviewing progress regularly (daily/weekly/monthly).

You won't need a detailed plan for every goal. For example, let's say your goal was to buy a puppy for a family pet. By talking with your family, you could determine the kind of puppy they wanted and decide on a budget. The final step would be purchasing the puppy at a pet store, through a want ad, or from the Humane Society. You could record this process, but it may be simpler to think it through. However, some goals require more details. Here's an example.

Goal	Action Steps	Progress Reviewed/ Results
To earn an extra $10,000 this year	1. Make four to five extra calls a day.	1. Each extra call has increased my income by $200 a week.
	2. Open two to three new accounts each week.	2. Five new accounts opened in two weeks.
	3. Write a proposal and sell major new account by April.	3. First draft completed.

Making more money is a more complex goal and will require more attention, time, and effort than buying a puppy. Apply these steps on the next few pages for your goals. Include at least one work-related goal. If you need more, feel free to copy the pages.

Note: Your strategic selling plan, done earlier, is your big-picture look at mining the gold in your territory or location. This goal-setting process is about the personal payoff for succeeding with your plan. Some of your action steps here can come from that strategic selling plan.

Goal Statement	
Action Steps	Timelines
1.	
2.	
3.	
4.	
5.	
6.	
7.	
8.	
9.	
10.	
11.	
Progress Review	

Goal Statement	
Action Steps	Timelines
1.	
2.	
3.	
4.	
5.	
6.	
7.	
8.	
9.	
10.	
11.	

Progress Review

Positive Affirmations

Henry Ford once said, "If you believe you can or you can't, you're right." All salespeople talk to themselves. It's called self-talk, and it occurs in your mind. Most of the time it includes negative thoughts. Affirmations are positive, deliberate thoughts, declarations, images, or feelings aimed to produce a desired result. Affirmations help you reprogram your mind; they are hopeful and optimistic statements and often start with "I am." Affirmations are peak-performance words you say to yourself to remain positive and on track toward your sales success.

Here are some examples:

▷ I am a loving parent and spouse.

▷ I am an excellent cook, and people enjoy my meals.

▷ I am filled with joy because I'm achieving my goals.

▷ I am in excellent shape.

▷ I know my market and my customers' needs.

▷ I am achieving and exceeding my sales goals.

▷ I am the best at _____.

Steps:

1. Write three affirmations (each) related to business and personal situations.

2. Get comfortable. Take a few deep breaths. Think of your job. State your affirmations.

3. Repeat your affirmations at least three times a day. Say them at times when you think about them and when you feel discouraged.

4. Know that affirmations are changing you now. It will take time to change old habits into new results. Add to your affirmation list.

Business	Personal
1.	1.
2.	2.
3.	3.

Mental Rehearsal

Visualizing includes mentally picturing your desired result. Mental rehearsal is another name for it. Carpenters use blueprints, advertisers use television, and a business uses a strategic plan. People use visualizations to imagine an idea's reality or their perfect future.

It's the master skill of peak performers. In sales, mental rehearsal is a great technique to prepare for a sales call, to visualize goal achievement, or to stay positive after a lost sale. Today this skill is taught to all premiere athletes—amateur and professional. Often, you will hear superstar athletes say in interviews, "I have imagined this many times before," or something along those lines.

You are a professional. Why would you do anything different to achieve the success you desire and live the life you dream about?

Steps to Mental Rehearsal
1.   Get comfortable and relax in a pleasant place.
2.   Close your eyes and think about one of your goals.
3.   Imagine achieving that goal.
4.   Picture a movie playing in your mind. The title is *Success in Achieving My Goal.*
5.   Note your feelings at the time of success. Notice other images, scents, sounds, or details in your mind.
6.   Repeat your affirmation with enthusiasm and excitement.
7.   Say thank you.
8.   Record your observations here.

Feelings?

Snapshot of the picture? Images?

Sounds? Scents? Details?

Physical surroundings?

Attitude?

DAY 27

Superstar Customer Service

So you want to deliver great customer service. What are your reasons?

▷ Make more money?

▷ Drive more sales?

▷ Surpass competitors?

▷ Refine your reputation?

▷ Attract the best employees?

Most companies ultimately want to make more money, and because every company makes money differently, the underlying objectives differ—even if the main motive is the same. Now, although money is great, customers can tell the difference between a company that's genuine and a company that's just going after the green. The key to making more green while making customers more satisfied is to convince them that you (your business) are irreplaceable. Think about it: If we take customer service out of the equation, there are many things you hear described as "the best." And what do you notice about places categorized as "the best"? They are chosen first and foremost over all other similar businesses, even if one factor of the business isn't as flawless as its leaders might hope.

Just to make sure we're on the same page: We've all been told (at one point or another) about someone else's idea of "the best" pizza place. Think back to that moment when someone told you where that was. Now, try to remember whether, when they told you, you asked how much the pizza cost. Did you ask how busy it was? Did you ask how great the service was? Did you get details on the cleanliness of the pizza joint? Did you ask what beverage options they had available?

The answer to each and every one of these questions is *no*. Does that mean price, service, cleanliness, and other details don't matter? Not at all. What it does demonstrate to you is that when a business separates itself as "the best" by whatever means, all of the other aspects fade into the background. It is only when a business isn't the best that these other components become critical to customers.

With all of that being said, it's your turn to determine how you plan to differentiate yourself as "the best" in whatever industry you play in. *The key is to intentionally identify the specific need of your niche.* Get to know your customers, their expectations, their preferences, and where else they go to get what you give out. Then, brainstorm. Either do something nobody else is doing or do something better than everyone else is doing it. Knowing where you need to start isn't always simple—but becoming "the best" at whatever it is you do, is always worthwhile. Once you get to this point, your customers, your employees, and your leaders will truly understand the value of priceless.

Know this: The best salespeople deliver the best service. They believe in the adage that sales and service both are all about meeting or exceeding customer needs. Truly, *excellent selling is excellent service and excellent service is excellent selling*. So now, tell us: *How do you attempt to become the best in the business?*

Sales Activity Reflection: Superstar Customer Service

Think of a business where you have spent money and received excellent customer service. What did they do that made them so good?

Outline your commitment to Superstar customer service.

Team Selling

Effective Team Selling

One of our major international clients (one that is well-known for its innovation and creativity) manufactures and sells its products to some of the largest companies in the world. It eventually began to get complaints from its customers because multiple sales professionals were regularly calling on the same customer. True, the sales professionals were representing different business units and were selling different products, but to the customer, this parade of salespeople often appeared disjointed and duplicative. The customers were, in fact, dealing with different customer service, billing, R & D, and engineering groups, as well as different salespeople, based on the products they were using. Even though this was all happening within the same organization, the sales professionals often didn't know who else was calling on the customer, nor could they solve problems for the customer if they were related to the products and services provided and managed by another business unit within their own company.

For another one of our clients, the pace of technological change and resulting new product introductions move at breakneck speeds. Its world headquarters is in Europe, and the U.S.–based organization has recently gone through a tremendous expansion with the intention of capturing a large chunk of U.S. market share. The business operates with a traditional organizational structure, with sales, customer service, professional product application trainers, marketing, and supply chain each operating as separate functions within the global structure. Of course, this means that the employees who do the work of each of these functions report to different supervisors and middle managers who are accountable to functional executives up the organizational ladder.

In both cases briefly outlined here, the employees in the customer's organization interact with the sales organization regularly to buy, apply, integrate, and use the products for certain applications, or they sell the product to their customers (end users). Each of these interactions contributes to the customer's experience and has the potential to add intelligence to the body of knowledge used by the sales professionals to sell in the future, and to maintain competitiveness in the marketplace. Each interaction takes time, costs money, and contributes value (or not), and in many cases has a positive or negative impact for the customer that frequently does not get communicated to the salesperson who manages the account. The sales professional may learn about it when the customer gets frustrated and calls to complain because a product wasn't shipped, or has quality problems upon receipt. Someone in the organization may have known about the problem previously and may have been working diligently to resolve it. When it becomes a customer problem, the search for blame becomes almost as prevalent as the search for solutions to resolve the issue. In an attempt to smooth over the problem and resolve the issues, it is not uncommon for one member of the organization to blame another person or group from his or her own organization. This does little to improve or maintain the customer relationship.

The Value of Team Selling

Both of these organizations have addressed these complex problems by shifting to a team-based selling model. The exact design of the teams varies according to the customer's needs, but many of the changes have similar threads. Here are some of the benefits of moving to team-based selling:

▷ With many different "touch points" in the customer organization, there is a much higher probability that the sales team will capture insight into opportunities that are emerging in the customer's business more quickly than in the traditional selling structure. Often the insight occurs in real time, as the customer is identifying needs or opportunities.

▷ The team has a much higher likelihood of gaining awareness of problems brewing or issues present among members of a customer's executive team or within the user organization.

▷ Trainers, customer service representatives, or technical support employees often are able to hear or see which members of the customer's organization view the product favorably and who has negative feelings or concerns about it.

▷ Members of the sales team often hear about or bump into changes in customer policy that affect their relationship with the customer much sooner than you would normally experience it (payment terms, quality problems, legal issues, restructuring, financial problems, and so forth).

▷ The more broadly your team is involved with the customer's organization, the more likely it is that team members will access knowledge of individuals who may be actively seeking alternatives to your product or company, or who may be seeking to replace you.

▷ If your team members hold allegiance to your team, you will be more likely to receive timely information when you're facing internal issues or problems that affect our ability to meet the customer's requirements (for example, quality, delivery, timeliness, and increased product defect rate).

▷ Likewise, you'll be more likely to tap into newly emerging information within your organization or the general marketplace that may affect your ability to be effective.

▷ Overall, you have the potential to eliminate unnecessary waste, improve your overall sales volume and effectiveness, and increase your profitability as a result.

To Be Effective

You'll need to assemble your team carefully and ensure that each team member has the skills and understanding of the importance of the sales team's effectiveness. Your sales effectiveness depends on your ability to create:

▷ Alignment of purpose.

▷ Alignment of effort.

▷ Commitment to success.

▷ Sense of responsibility and accountability.

▷ Personal skin in the game.

What Is Required?

Common Vision of Success

The change to a team-based selling process must be carefully thought through and carefully communicated. It will be helpful to talk about the problems faced by continuing the current selling approach as well as the expected benefits of moving to the team-based approach. Customer satisfaction, improved efficiencies, reduced duplication, easier problem resolution, broader access to important customer information, mutual support, and many other very real benefits need to be discussed and turned into elements of the vision for success. A common vision for success is essential to the team's ability to turn this very significant organizational change into reality.

Clarity of Purpose

Every member of the team needs to shift their allegiance from their functional area of responsibility to an allegiance centered on the team's success. That is, they must now take on personal responsibility for the team's sales success and for the customer's satisfaction with the company as a whole. The purpose of everyone's job now centers on the success of the team's sales. They are now individually and collectively accountable for sales and service results. The questions that must be answered include:

▷ What are we seeking to accomplish, and how important is it?

▷ What impact does it have on our customer?

▷ How does our organization benefit from success here? How do each of us benefit from success?

Goals

The vision and purposes must be expressed as clear goals:

▷ What are our measures of success?

▷ How does each of us contribute to that?

▷ How will each of us and all of us know how we're doing in pursuit of our success?

Clear Roles

The team needs to get clear about what work needs to be done and who is best suited to do it. They need to learn roles are bigger than job descriptions. The team needs to discuss and get clear about what part each person plays in the overall coordination of required, tasks, effort, and output, and how that impacts the customer's success.

Effective Procedures

The team will need to decide how it will coordinate efforts and information to accomplish the goals that are set. Often the procedures include things like:

- ▷ How will we communicate, and how frequently?
- ▷ How will we uncover problems and issues that need to be discussed, solved, and managed for success?
- ▷ What tools do we need?
- ▷ What skills do we need to develop to be successful?

Effective Interpersonal Relationships

The team's success will depend on what we do and how we do it. The quality of the team's relationships with our customers and with one another will determine much of the team's success. Coming together over boundaries and values about how we will work together will help the team move through difficult problems, engage in problem-solving, and, eventually, mature into a well-oiled and effective team that represents the company well and that meets customer expectations for success.

Sales Activity Reflection: Team-Based Selling

1. Write a brief list of performance indicators you see that suggest to you that your "customer-facing" organization may not be working as effectively as it should.

2. Identify the opportunities you see that may be better realized if your sales effort was provided by a well-orchestrated team.

3. What steps do you see that need to be taken to determine if a team-based sales effort is right for your organization?

- Who else needs to be involved in making this decision?

- What kinds of training need to be considered before a team-based structure could reasonably be expected to succeed in your organization?

What Is Your Customers' Experience?

When salespeople think "customer experience," they can easily form certain assumptions and come to certain conclusions about what that means. If a sales rep (or the company he works for) hasn't defined who his customer "really" is or what differentiated value he adds with his product or service, he is headed for serious market challenges. Sales professionals today must be proactive in improving their company's interactions with the customer, including their own sales practices. Any company needs to do this to survive and thrive today. Don't wait for your company to get focused on the customer; you do it! Bottom line, if you don't do this, you risk discounting the importance of customer service, losing customer loyalty, and decreasing your income.

We all have a pretty little bow tied around our simple little idea that customer service either involves a telephone rep or a checkout line, when in reality, the majority of customer experiences fall far outside of these two elements.

Here's the key point for most sales reps: The "customer service" their customers receive determines the extent of their repeat business.

If you're struggling to get a good sense of your customers' experience, do a thorough analysis of your answers to these questions. We encourage the whole sales team in companies to do this and then look for ways to help the company improve.

1. At what point is our department intersecting with others?
2. What happens at this point of connection for both parties with the customer?
3. What various factors in sales do we control that could alter the customers' experience?

4. What external factors could influence the customers' experience that we *can* control?

5. How will we manage these factors to ensure they work to our benefit?

6. What external factors could influence the customers' experience that we *can't* control?

7. Do we have any resources that will help us manage these uncontrollable factors?

8. What are the steps of your company's defined customer experience?

9. How many employees play a role in that process?

10. Do all of these employees know their roles and responsibilities in the experience?

If these questions seem step-by-step, it's intentional. The best way to get into the customers' shoes is to experience each moment as it happens. From the minute your customers hear, see, feel or become aware of your business, they are experiencing your business. Don't look at your numbers and make assumptions; walk the customers' way to really get into their world.

Sales Activity Reflection: What Is Your Customers' Experience?

What are the strengths of your organization based on these questions?

What are the weaknesses of your organization based on these questions?

How can you help your organization improve?

A Review: Superstar Selling Action Plan

Congratulations! You are nearing the end of this 31-day learning effort. You have covered a great deal of information, and, with the help of the reflections and action planning steps, you have clarified your thinking and identified opportunities for additional development of your knowledge and skills. Now you're moving into the action planning stage of Superstar selling that will help you to carry your learning opportunities forward throughout your career. We know that new knowledge alone will not last long, as the press of your daily activity and the need to take on new information will push much of what you have learned out of your long-term memory—that is, unless you commit yourself to actions that will reinforce your knowledge and support your long-term maintenance of your new skills. Take some time with this next application to identify the new knowledge you have gained from reading this book, as well as the specific ways you can and will apply that knowledge to your day-to-day work activities. Doing so will help you maintain this new knowledge and, indeed, continue to develop it further.

Learning	Application
What did you learn or relearn about being more customer-centered?	How will you apply this to your sales activities?
What did you learn or relearn about Superstar selling strategies?	How will you apply this to your sales activities?
What did you learn or relearn about pre-call planning and sales documentation?	How will you apply this to your sales activities?
What did you learn or relearn about emotional resiliency?	How will you apply this to your position?

Learning	Application
In summary, identify four to six selling strengths.	How will you apply these strengths more often?
In summary, identify two to three areas to improve.	How will you take action in these areas?

Your best success will occur if you take the specific actions you've identified and transfer them as action steps in your daily calendar plans. The more you practice and take action, the more the new information, skills, and strategies will become a part of you.

Managing Time for Superstar Results

Talent, information, and desire are not enough to be successful in sales. Changes in self-perception and behavior are required, especially when implementing new techniques and ideas. That's what we have been working on throughout *Superstar Sales.* But don't worry: Big changes aren't usually required. It's the little things that make a difference. Everyone has comfort zones and blind spots. Sometimes, we miss the obvious. Read the sentence aloud in each illustration that follows.

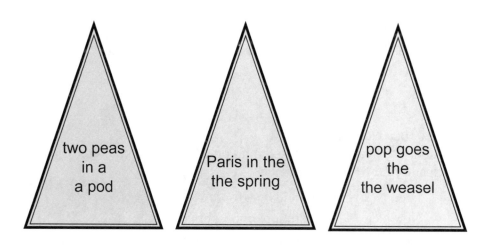

Did you just read the sentences as you remembered them? Notice each has an extra word (a, the, the). Most people don't see this the first time. This is another example of our mental models. What are you missing that's right in front of you? Sometimes, it's an idea, a solution to a current problem, or an answer to future sales. What you need is often in front of you, but you don't see or use it. Why? It happens to everyone. It has to do with the blinders you have on, which are caused by the beliefs you've accepted over the years, beliefs such as:

> ▷ I can't change!
> ▷ I am what I am!
> ▷ I'm not that kind of person.
> ▷ That's just me.
> ▷ I always do it this way; it has worked before.
> ▷ Why do I need to do it when others don't?

Everyone has problems and potential built-in resistant behaviors; however, Superstars are more willing to change and try new things to get different results. When it makes sense, they shed old habits and beliefs as naturally as leaves fall from trees in autumn. You can't really manage time because it's constant, but you can manage yourself! Successful self-management requires you to continue learning as you have in this book and to:

> ▷ Expand your comfort zone.
> ▷ Establish positive beliefs.
> ▷ Increase your productivity.
> ▷ Be satisfied with your life.

Expand Your Comfort Zone

All of us have self-imposed limitations. Don't be a creature of habit. To expand your potential, you need:

> ▷ Feedback—positive and negative. Ask for it!
> ▷ New ideas. Try different methods; brainstorm!
> ▷ Failures. Andrew Carnegie said the way to succeed is to fail more often.
> ▷ Change. Make a new habit and stay with it for 30 days.

Establish Positive Beliefs

Don't you want to increase your sales performance, energy, and success? Never forget that talent, knowledge, and desire aren't enough to achieve what you want. You have to change your beliefs. Your beliefs shape your attitude. Your attitude determines how you use your talent, knowledge, and dreams—all of which determine your actions. Here's how to establish positive beliefs:

1. Maintain a positive focus. It sounds simple, but psychologists tell us that 85 percent of our thoughts are negative.[1]

2. Mentally rehearse. Pre-play positive results for sales, goals, and customer contacts.

3. Try self-talk and positive affirmations. Take time to put positive words in your mind. Positive in, positive out (PIPO)—not garbage in, garbage out (GIGO).

Try affirmations as we have discussed, such as:

▷ I am an excellent salesperson.

▷ I am healthy and fit.

▷ I communicate well and with sincerity.

Review your own affirmations regularly. Make them personal, in the present tense, and positive.

Practice: Expand and Establish

To apply these two concepts immediately, complete the following activities and write about your experience in the space provided.

> • Solicit feedback from a coworker. Specify that you'd like him or her to give you at least one positive point of feedback and one constructive point of feedback.

- Brainstorm a list of five things you could change in your daily work routine.

- List two failures you've had in life that led to great things.

- Identify three habits you would like to change. Choose one that you want to focus on doing differently for the next three days.

- List five things you would like to think about yourself. Choose one that you will repeat to yourself at least five times today.

- Write about your experience doing these activities here.

Increase Your Productivity

Many salespeople spend most of their time responding to fires and chaos. Not enough time is spent talking to customers, planning, learning, and following up. Your payoff activities involve these functions. Be a pro and find time to complete these activities. Eliminate the word *can't* and, in the words of Winston Churchill, "never give up; never, never give up."[2]

Implement these peak-performance techniques:

1. Follow a personal-management system for organizing, scheduling, goal-tracking, and time-management purposes. Most cell phones today have apps to help with this. Most laptops or desktops have tools for this, as well. Franklin Planners also has proven tools. Each should include these key elements:

   ▷ Annual and monthly calendar overview.

   ▷ Daily calendar (to-do list, calls, and appointments).

   ▷ Contacts.

   ▷ Goals.

   ▷ Important data.

   ▷ Notes.

   Find one planner and use it. Don't use two or three; you'll be ineffective. Also, if it's important, write it down (meeting, idea, activity, goal). Test this concept in a personal planner, and you'll truly save an hour a day.

2. Write down your goals and action plans. Again, if it isn't written down, it's not important to you. All great achievers are great planners. Opportunities prefer the prepared mind.

3. Keep learning. Read, listen to CDs, and take courses on management. No matter how successful you are now, you will only limit yourself if you stop learning.

Be Satisfied With Your Life

Live each moment to the fullest. It's important to plan for the future and to get things done; however, it's easy to get trapped by a whirlwind and never enjoy or appreciate who you are or what is really important. Though we want to succeed in sales, what is the success really for? Remember these five great ideas:

▷ Nurture your relationships.

▷ Take care of your spiritual needs.

▷ Help others in need.

▷ Find alone time.

▷ Do nothing sometimes.

Does thou love life? Then don't squander time. It's the stuff life is made of.

—Benjamin Franklin

Sales Activity Reflection: Increase Productivity and Satisfaction

To apply these two concepts immediately, complete the following activities and write about your experience in the space provided.

• Identify the peak-performance technique you currently use most often, or determine why you don't currently use a technique.
• Identify the peak-performance technique that might make more sense for you personally, and review why it makes more sense for you to use.
• Determine three to five steps you will take to put your peak-performance technique into practice. In other words, determine what you will need to do between now and then to implement a technique successfully.

- Brainstorm a list of 10 things that are important to you.

- List five things you would like to devote more time to enjoying.

- List five things you currently make time to do that you would like to reevaluate.

Final Reflection: Your Superstar Selling Experience

Use this space to reflect on your experience reading, engaging, and interacting with the stories, activities, and information in *Superstar Sales*. Pay special attention to your feelings, thoughts, goals, or ideas. This is a valuable page to reference from time to time. It can serve as a reminder, a motivator, a passion-starter, or proof that you always had the potential to be a Superstar!

Notes

Introduction
1. "Closing the Sale: Salespeople's Choices Are the Key," First Concepts Consultants Inc. Website (2012). *www.firstconcepts.com/closing-the-sale/*.
2. Chen, Feng-Chi, and Wen-Hsiung Li. "Genomic Divergences between Humans and Other Hominoids and the Effective Population Size of the Common Ancestor of Humans and Chimpanzees." *American Journal of Human Genetics 68(2)*: 444–456 (February 2001).

   For more information Human Genome Project, visit *ornl.gov/sci/techresources/Human_Genome/home.shtml*.

How to Use This Book
1. "Optimism-Pessimism Assessed in the 1960s and Self-Reported Health Status 30 Years Later," *Mayo Clinic Proceedings, Volume 77, Issue 8*: 748–753 (August 2002).

Chapter 3
1. "Optimism-Pessimism."

Chapter 4
1. Leighton, Tim. "Minnesota High School Basketball's Top Scorer Anders Broman: 4,381 and Counting," *St. Paul Pioneer Press,* January 15, 2013.

Chapter 10
1. Ungerleider, Steven. "Visions of Victory," *Psychology Today* (1992).
2. Hess, Karl. "How to Save Strokes in Every Round," *Milwaukee Examiner* Web site (July 19, 2009), *www.examiner.com/article/how-to-save-strokes-every-round*.
3. Raffel, Shaun. "Realistic Training: Optional Extra or Core Skill?" Scribd Web site, *www.scribd.com/doc/115194556/REALISTIC-TRAINING-Optional-Extra-or-Core-Skill-by-Shan-Raffel-EngTech-MIFireE*.
4. "The Power of Imagination," Abundanceandhappiness.com (2012), *www.abundance-and-happiness.com/power-of-imagination.html*.

Chapter 15

1. To find this quote or to learn more about Amelia Earhart, visit the official Website: *www.ameliaearhart.com.*

Chapter 16

1. If you'd like to learn more about the importance of points of contact in sales, here are a few sources we found to be insightful:

   Corry, Will. "80% of Sales Occur after the 5th Contact," The Marketingblog Extra Web site (July 4, 2011), *wcorry.blogspot. com/2011/07/new-guaranteed-position-package-and.html.*

   "How Do You Jump Ahead of the Crowd by 80%," SaaS Expert Web site (June 23, 2009), *coollifesystems.wordpress.com/2009/06/23/ how-do-you-jump-ahead-of-the-crowd-by-80/.*

   Zahrte, Bill. "80% of Sales," Automotive Dealers Network Web site (n.d.), *www.automotivedealersnetwork.com/Articles/ BillZahrte/80PercentOfSales.html.*

2. Koneya, Mele, and Alton Barbour. *Louder Than Words: Non-Verbal Communication* (Interpersonal Communication Series, Merrill, 1976).

Chapter 20

1. Whittenberg, Michael. *The Great Debate: Who Are the Top 10 Players in NBA History?* BleacherReport.com (2008).

Chapter 21

1. Galorath, Dan. "Software Project Failure Costs Billions. Better Estimation & Planning Can Help," SEER Galorath Web site (June 7, 2012), *www.galorath .com/wp/software-project-failure-costs-billions-better-estimation-planning-can-help.php.*

Chapter 22

1. Lucado, Max. *In the Eye of the Storm* (World Publishing, 1991), *bible.org/ illustration/courageous-candidate.*

2. Garfield, Charles. *The New Heroes in American Business* (New York: William Morrow Paperbacks, 1987).

3. Waitley, Dr. Denis. *The Psychology of Winning* (New York: Penguin, 1986).

Chapter 31

1. We found this study on optimism/pessimism extremely insightful. You can learn more here: Tindle, H., et al. "Optimism, Cynical Hostility, and Incident Coronary Heart Disease and Mortality in the Women's Health Initiative," *Circulation 120(8)*: 656–662 (August 25, 2009).

2. After the Blitz in World War II, Winston Churchill made this legendary statement in his speech at Harrow School on October 29, 1941.

Index

About the Authors

Doug Watsabaugh, COO/Cofounder

Doug values being a regular person, with his feet on the ground and head in the realities of the daily challenges his clients face. It's his heart for and experience in helping clients deal with difficult situations that distinguish him from other sales performance and leadership development consultants.

His knowledge of experiential learning, and his skill at designing change processes and learning events have enabled him to measurably improve the lives of thousands of individuals and hundreds of organizations in a wide variety of industries—financial services, manufacturing, medical devices, consumer goods, and technology, to name a few.

Before starting his own business, Doug served as the director of operations for a national training institute, served as manager of organization development for a major chemical company, and was responsible for worldwide training and organization development for the world's third-largest toy company.

He was also a partner in Performance & Human Development LLC, a California company that published high-involvement experiential activities, surveys and instruments, interactive training modules, papers, and multimedia presentations.

Doug has coauthored two books with John E. Jones, PhD, and William L. Bearley, EdD: *The New Fieldbook for Trainers* (HRD Press and Lakewood Publishing) and *The OUS Quality Item Pool,* about organizational survey items that measure Baldrige criteria. His newest book, coauthored with Rick Conlow, is *Superstar Leadership.*

He is a member of the American Society for Training and Development (ASTD), the Minnesota Quality Council, and the National Organization Development Network.

Doug's father taught him the value of hard work, and it paid dividends: He funded his college education playing guitar and singing with a rock 'n' roll band, experiencing a close call with fame when he played bass in concert with Chuck Berry—not bad for a guy who admits to being a bit shy.

Though Doug's guitar remains a source of enjoyment, it pales in comparison to his number-one joy and priority: his family.

Rick Conlow, CEO/Cofounder

There aren't many who'd argue the fact that Rick is one enthusiastic and results-oriented guy. Even the titles of his books, articles, speeches, and initiatives reflect his drive and positive energy.

A quick glance at his professional resume leaves you with the strong impression that effort and optimism are a winning combination. Case in point: With Rick by their side, clients have achieved double- and triple-digit improvement in their sales performance, quality, customer loyalty, and service results during the past 20-plus years, and have earned more than 30 quality and service awards.

In a day and age when optimism and going the extra mile can sound trite, Rick has made them differentiators. His clients include organizations that are leaders in their industries, as well as others that are less recognizable. Regardless, their goals are his goals. Whereas many consultants talk about consistent and sustainable results, Rick helps his clients achieve them.

Rick's life view and extensive background in sales and leadership—as a general manager, vice president, training director, program director, national sales trainer, business owner, and management consultant—are the foundation of his coaching, training, and consulting services. Participants in Rick's experiential, live-action programs walk away with "ah-ha's," inspiration, and skills they can immediately use.

These programs include "BEST Selling!" "SuperSTAR Customer Service," "Excellence in Management!" "SuperSTAR Selling!" "The Greatest Secrets of all Time!" "The State of the Art in Improving the Customer Experience," and "SuperSTAR Leadership, Good Boss/Bad Boss—Which One Are You?"

Rick has also authored *Excellence in Management, Excellence in Supervision, SuperSTAR Customer Service, SuperSTAR Selling, Designing a SuperSTAR Customer Experience, SuperSTAR Leadership,* and *Returning to Learning.* He and his business partner, Doug Watsabaugh, have published six new books together. Their newest book is *Superstar Leadership.*

When he's not engaging an audience or engrossed in a coaching discussion, this proud husband and father is most likely astride a weight bench or a motorcycle taking on the back roads and highways of any state.

About WCW Partners

Results Realized. Goals Exceeded.

▷ Who We Are

WCW Partners is a management consulting and training company. Based in Minneapolis/St. Paul, Minnesota, we work with clients in a variety of industries worldwide to help them excel in sales, service, and leadership. We facilitate business growth and vitality through four practices: sales and customer-retention improvement, organization and leadership development, innovation, and communications strategy.

▷ Our Approach

We don't mind telling you that we're different than most consulting firms you'll find in the marketplace. For one thing, it's our approach—when you hire us, you get us. But just as important, we're people who've had to wrestle with the same issues you have—how to strengthen sales, boost productivity, improve quality, increase employee satisfaction, build a team, or retain and attract new customers. To us, "We develop the capability in you" is more than a catchy phrase; it's our promise.

▷ Our Experience

Our clients include 3M, American Express, American Medical Systems, Amgen Inc., Accenture, AmeriPride Services, Andersen Windows, Avanade, Beltone, Canadian Linen and Uniform Service, Carew International, Case Corporation, Citigroup, Coca-Cola, Costco, Covance, Deknatel, Eaton Corporation, Electrochemicals Inc., Entergy, Esoterix, General Mills, GN Resound, Grant Thornton, Hasbro Inc., Honeywell, Interton, Kenner Products, Loews Financial, Northern Power, Marketlink, Kemps-Marigold, Meijer Corporation, National Computer

Systems, Parker Brothers, Target, Toro, Productive Workplace Systems, Red Wing Shoes, Rite Aid, Rollerblade, Ryan Companies, Travelers Insurance, Thrivent, Tonka Corporation, Widex, and a number of nonprofit and educational institutions.

▷ Our Success

We have helped companies achieve: 8%-plus gains in retail sales growth in a tough market, 5–7% gains in transaction counts, 57% reduction in customer complaints, 75% gain in sales to existing customers, 53% improvement in sales, 34 quality and customer service awards, Ford's President's Award, the JD Power Award for Service, and much, much more.

▷ Contact Us

To learn how you can do amazing things, visit us online at *www. wcwpartners.com* or contact Doug or Rick toll free at (888) 313–0514.